D0007419

The Students Are Watching

Edited by Nancy Faust Sizer and Theodore R. Sizer
Five Lectures on Moral Education (1970)

By Nancy Faust Sizer
Making Decisions: Cases for Moral Discussion (1984)
China: Tradition and Change (1979, 1991)

By Theodore R. Sizer
Places for Learning, Places for Joy: Speculations on American School Reform (1973)
Horace's Compromise: The Dilemma of the American High School (1984)
Horace's School: Redesigning the American High School (1992)
Horace's Hope: What Works for the American High School (1996)

THE

Schools and the Moral Contract

STUDENTS

Theodore R. Sizer

ARE

Nancy Faust Sizer

WATCHING

Beacon Press · Boston

BEACON PRESS
25 Beacon Street
Boston, Massachusetts 02108-2892
www.beacon.org

Beacon Press books are published under the auspices of
the Unitarian Universalist Association of Congregations.

05   04   03   02   01   00   99   8   7   6   5   4   3   2

This book is printed on recycled acid-free paper that contains at least
20 percent postconsumer waste and meets the uncoated paper ANSI/NISO
specifications for permanence as revised in 1992.

Text design by Christopher Kuntze
Composition by Wilsted & Taylor Publishing Services

Library of Congress Cataloging-in-Publication Data

Sizer, Theodore R.
    The students are watching : schools and the moral contract /
Theodore R. Sizer, Nancy Faust Sizer.
        p.   cm.
    ISBN 0-8070-3120-8
    1. Moral education (Secondary)—United States.   2. Teacher-student
relationships—United States.   3. High school teachers—United
States.   4. Education, Secondary—Aims and objectives—United
States.   5. Effective teaching—United States.   I. Sizer, Nancy
Faust.   II. Title.
LC311.S548   1999
373.1102'3—dc21   98-50171

For Our Grandchildren

May their schools deserve them!

Our whole life is startlingly moral.
There is never an instant's truce
between virtue and vice.

HENRY DAVID THOREAU

Contents

A MIDDLE-CLASS teacher and her working-class student face each other in a large, drafty, grimy high school. The walls had been a bilious green once, before they acquired so many smudges that they took on a dappled look. The stairs are basically sturdy, but broken-off linoleum makes them unsafe. The floors have not been swept thoroughly in a long time.

The student says, "You have been to college and stuff. What are *you* doing in a dump like this?"

He has accepted the message that such a high school conveys: You kids deserve to be neglected, to be surrounded by a blatant lack of respect. Besides an ugly, out-of-date building, you will have inadequate supplies, large classes, and many transient or substitute teachers who have been given the impression that it is their job to babysit rather than to teach. He sees no way out of such a "dump" for himself. But he can not see why she would choose even to come to such a place, let alone to work in it. He's a bit suspicious. Is she here just to spy on him, to criticize the school? Another "hit and run" visitor interested only in research or some kind of exposé?

What can the teacher reply to a question like this? That she considers him her fellow American, her fellow human being? That she feels that by working in a "difficult" high school she will be able to help to make it better? That it matters less to her what the walls are like than what the people are like? That she needs, for her own sake, to find out if she has what it takes to teach him?

He is watching her, waiting for her answer, and she had better not be patronizing, but she had better not be dishonest either. She had better put not just words but also deeds at his disposal. She had better work not just as a teacher but as an activist within the school to create the kind of environment which would indicate society's respect for such a young person as he is.

While she will not achieve a miracle, she will make a difference. She will try to help him to grow into a decent and knowledgeable and principled person, thoughtfully weighing his options and choosing the ones which lead to long-term benefits for himself and others. Many of her colleagues will work in the same spirit, and as teachers they will overcome, for some of the students some of the time, the dappled walls and lack of books. Students such as this young man will notice their testament, and appreciate it, some for all their lives. Mr. Holland's Opus: corny but true.

Still, how long will the middle-class teacher last in such a school before she thinks about her other options? How long before she comes to feel as if she, too, is a piece of trash? How long will the nation tolerate the fact that so many of its children are being educated in "dumps"?

Even more than idealistic individuals and adequate money are needed, however. People teach, but the institutions which people build also teach. If the high school is impersonal, if its message is boring and its goals are out of date, if its methods seem heartless and even vindictive, the students will learn from that too. It is the mores, the routines, the ways of schools which we want to consider in this book. The adults in American high schools are bad and good, sensitive and inhumane. Indeed, many are generous on Wednesday and stingy on Thursday, and such will always be. It is not enough to recruit better teachers. We must insist on a high school design which will help all the high school's people to reach for the best version of themselves.

What we need—as teachers, as parents and grandparents, as citizens and taxpayers—to consider and then to create is the kind of environment which will hold its best teachers by convincing youngsters like this young man that he is in a place which believes in him—and from which he can, therefore, learn well and deeply. What he can learn is Spanish and biology, algebra and literature, but also to be a young man who believes in his own moral agency, his capacity to make wise decisions and then act on them even when he is faced with all the temptations life will inevitably provide.

R AISING UP decent and principled children has been the desire of humankind for millennia. The great texts in most traditions have been moral tracts, guidebooks to inform and storybooks to inspire the young with worthy models to emulate.

Many of these tracts arise from terror of the unknown, from the uncertainty of why we exist, what will happen to us, what the meaning of our fragile living signifies.

Rarely is the terror forthrightly admitted. The focus of energy is on the mechanisms a society erects to protect civilization, mechanisms which reflect and project the social norms that guard against (or are believed to guard against) a descent into what literal seventeenth-century settlers on these shores called barbarism. Three such mechanisms have characterized most civilizations—the family or clan, religion, and education. A fourth is the mass media, so new in its extraordinary reach that there are few norms for its conduct.

Modern American society tinkers with families and clans only at the extreme margins. The life of a family is largely protected and private, with the community invading only when it suspects intolerable neglect or cruelty. The American church is both neglected—it too is protected space—and idealized. Religion is sanctioned; for example, our coins tell us that "In God We Trust." The media are still considered primarily a business, and thus are left "free" of cultural regulation and required to defend their existence by means of a monetary rather than a cultural bottom line.

That leaves education. American young people must by law attend a state-sanctioned school for at least ten years, a requirement—utterly accepted as a norm by contemporary Americans—that is the most remarkable imposition of state power that most citizens ever experience. With the family and the church largely off limits and the media left to commerce, public attention focuses on the schools. They become a sturdy vehicle for community cohesion, a cultural battleground, and often both at once.

Every decade yields its particular crop of books on "moral education." Most arise more or less from the discipline of philosophy. Increasingly we study as a matter of behavioral science the ways that young people apparently develop their values and the habits that reflect these values. "Moral education" has become its own scholarly discipline, involving detailed analyses of means as well as ends. In and around the schools, while the sermon on morality persists, it has been joined by more psychologically tailored approaches. Educators and public philosophers tinker incessantly with the ways that schooling can shape enduring moral habits.

A problem with "moral education" as it is presently undertaken, especially in middle and high schools, is that the matter is most often framed as a collection of nouns. Impressive nouns. Absolutes, even. There is a shimmering intensity and a fixed quality to concepts such as respect, integrity, and honesty which make them hard to reach for, let alone attain. Paradoxically, they gain sturdiness from this elusiveness. Either one tells the truth or one doesn't. Good character is personified by George Washington and the done-in cherry tree. Start here, and you will not go wrong.

But for other reasons good character often involves shaving the truth. "Mom, I can't go to the party with this big zit on my nose. Everyone will notice it. They'll make fun of me . . ." "Oh no, it's not so bad. Put some cream on it. No one will notice . . . You'll be just fine." Reality is that the zit will shed the cream, it is large and ugly, some people will notice it and look beyond it, others will notice it and sympathize, and yet others will make cruel fun of it. Mom knew this would be the case. She was deliberately dishonest, making a judgment because of her belief in a greater good: people have to learn to live with physical imperfections, however trifling; to get her daughter to the party to learn this fact required knowingly making an unrealistic prediction of what might happen there; the costs to the daughter's ego would likely be less than the gains in the daughter's realization that zits don't make the woman. Few would say that Mom was immoral in her deliberate (however trivial) deceit.

But deceit is still deceit. Situations do not always dictate principled conduct. Seriously considering nouns and adopting the most compelling of them as one's guideposts are laudable goals, surely; but such a strategy may also seem an impossible dream to those starting out, one so impossible that it is jettisoned in all but rhetoric. Too many of us just say the words and, confronted with the enormity of their meaning, wink away their application in practice. We honor truth until it suits us to keep a secret; we honor the highway laws until it suits us to speed. Nouns alone clearly don't work.

We have come to prefer verbs. They offer perspectives not seen in nouns. *Morality* itself, for example becomes *to moralize* when it is turned into a verb, and the differences are striking. There is superiority and condescension in the verb, and yet it still turns on the usefully rigid meaning of its parent noun.

There is wisdom to be found in examining differences such as that between "morality" and "moralizing." Nouns are treated as completed statues lined up on the top shelves of a person's character. Verbs are active, no less demanding but requiring constant engagement. They are not structures but, rather, engines. Reaching after morality needs to be a reflective process, built into the activities of each young person and the activities of that person's community, including the school—a process of stretching, of defining, of putting into context, of recognizing patterns, of testing, of feeling exhilaration or remorse. As Zen Buddhists say, it is the quality of the journey more than its destination which is to be celebrated. The destination is represented by a worthy noun. The journey functions as a verb. Both are essential. This book is primarily about the latter.

Between the two of us we have almost forty years of experience as teachers and administrators in public and private secondary schools here and in Australia. In addition to those schools where we have worked, we have visited hundreds of others over the last twenty years, here and abroad. We have listened and watched carefully and our experience informs this book. It reflects seasoned judgments rather than "findings" per se. It depends heavily on stories, all of which as rendered here are fictional but draw from a single or a clutch of actual experiences. Our depictions are not "real" but to our eyes they are not only "realistic" but helpfully representative. The book also builds on over four decades of conversation about a subject of intense joint interest between wife and husband. We respect the enormity of our topic; our hoped-for contribution is but a sliver of the matter.

T*HEY watch us all the time.* The students, that is. They listen to us, sometimes. They learn from all that watching and listening. Be quiet. Don't cheat. Pick up. Don't lie. Be nice. Don't fight. They attend to us, more than we usually realize. We yell to get the cafeteria quiet—a delicious irony, not lost on them—and we whisper to a child who is embarrassed but who needs to talk. We assign books that we have not read carefully ourselves and waste our students' time, or else together we discover an exciting new resource. We can be messy—just try to find last week's tests on the top of my desk—or as well organized as we ask our students to be.

We, who ask our students to use their minds well, can be pretty sloppy thinkers ourselves. Of course the valedictorian is smarter than the salutatorian: can't you see it in their course grades and test scores? Yet we realize that who is "smart" is a very controversial matter. And it is we who convince the student who believed that she was dumb that, in fact, she can write a convincing essay.

Some of us are unprofessional. We talk down our colleagues within earshot of the students, or even directly to them. "Oh, wow, you have Mrs. Graham [rolled eyes]. Can you switch out next term?" Yet in our isolated "egg-crate" profession, more and more of us are learning how to help each other and to create schools which have a lasting commitment to a better way of running themselves. The students are watching that too.

We can be selfish. If an institution claims to be responsive to a variety of constituencies but essentially serves only one, then it becomes hypocritical. Many teachers think of what their students need, but others have come to be content with thinking of what they need. It is true that teachers need to feel comfortable in order to serve children well, but how comfortable?

We are fallible, and should not pretend that we are anything else. But we ought to be aware of what we are doing. We have a profound moral contract with our students. We insist, under the law, that they become thoughtful, informed citizens. We must—for their benefit and ours—model such citizenship. The routines and rituals of a school teach, and teach especially about matters of character. A revealing way to observe those routines and rituals is through the lens provided by verbs, more specifically gerunds. Modeling. Grappling. Bluffing. Sorting. Shoving. Fearing.

They describe the actions of humans over millennia. The fear of barbarism which so animated our forebears is still there, even though we today may mask it with easier, softer language. All of us still struggle to be "civilized," and we need institutions which will nurture our humanity.

In the end, we teachers and other adults who care about children should attend to even the humblest of these actions and these dangers, so that we may teach our students—and ourselves—a worthy way of life.

The Students Are Watching

1 *Modeling*

"I'VE DECIDED one thing, anyway," Dave says. "I don't want to be an American. As soon as I get the chance, I'm leaving."

Dave arrives early to social studies class, and while he seemingly throws these words into the air, he clearly intends for the teacher to pick them up. A few of the kids hear them too.

Clearly Dave is not kidding. His sentiment is as genuine as it is unexpected, at least by his peers. Something serious is festering within him.

"Really? Why?" Ms. Santos's voice is calm, interested.

"Oh, I don't know, all these problems. You know . . . we talk about them all the time in this class. Americans think they are so great. We think we have the answers to everything, that everyone should copy us. I don't want to live in a place that's only thought of as rich and powerful. Especially when it's not really a democracy. I mean, there are way too many poor people, and how come so many of them are black? Other countries are better. I'll just go live in one of them."

Dave is going through the First Disillusion, a rite of passage that history teachers learn to expect. He's been through the whole Aren't-We-Americans-Just-Dandy curriculum, the one for little kids, and now he is learning about how hard it has been for his country to live up to its ideals. In him, however, the reaction is intense, more than passive awareness. His voice reveals how upset he is, even more than his words do.

"Do you have a country in mind, Dave?" Ms. Santos says. While class technically is to begin, she stays with Dave. The others watch, intrigued by all this painful honesty from their buddy.

As a matter of fact, Dave does have some countries in mind, but when he suggests two or three, the other kids mention problems in those countries too. It is a lively but not threatening discussion. Dave holds his own, but he increasingly appears ready to listen to others' views. Ms. Santos does not take part as the various facts are traded back and forth. The clock keeps ticking. Class is about Dave.

"Do you want to live in a country without problems?" Again her voice is quiet, her interest focused. The question, directed to Dave, embraces the others as well. All are intent. And in this round of the conversation, the teacher helps the students to consider the potential value of spending a life in a country where there is absorbing and worthy work to do. They catch on, and start giving examples of people they know, people thay have studied or read about who have been able to accomplish something—Eleanor Roosevelt, Martin Luther King, Cesar Chavez. After a while, Dave is able to come up with an example too. His voice grows less anguished. The issue—what is America like for the adults who live there?—becomes more complex.

"Class" should have started ten minutes ago. The other students are milling around, impatient with all this soul-searching and about to get into trouble. Ms. Santos shuts down the discussion of Dave's dilemma and the class moves back to Jacob Riis and the social troubles of the 1890s. She tells Dave, "Let's keep talking about this."

In the course of the conversation, the teacher is subtly guiding her students to see the ways in which honest and constructive adults make important personal decisions. They don't shy away from the pain they feel when they see things they don't like. They don't jump to conclusions before they have looked at further evidence. They keep their ultimate goals firmly in mind, especially the goal of a worthy life.

Ms. Santos is modeling that process by honoring Dave's dilemma. Her calmness in the face of Dave's anger implies that moral outrage is an acceptable emotion. It indicates that others—perhaps even she herself—have faced the decision that Dave is facing, and that they have found a way to deal with it. She shows that she realizes that such conversations and work take time: some now, some later. The way she responds implies that although moral outrage is understandable in the short run, it is also honorable to work to solve a problem. She is showing how it can be done—modeling—but she is also teaching, by carefully leading others through a process which is familiar to her.

Dave is still resolved to check out another nationality for himself. He is thinking hard, acting much less out of pain. He is at the time in his life when he is more likely to bring up agonizing personal dilemmas with his teacher than with his parents. If he were to tell them, at fifteen, that he was checking out other nationalities for himself, their reaction would be likely to be a mix of astonishment and ridicule. They would ignore his statement, or tell him he would outgrow it, or tell him stories about people who tried to emigrate and failed at it, or tell him that he needs to stay nearer home. They would be either in denial or in hysterics. Neither parent would coolly help Dave to walk through his impressions, convictions, and disappointment in America. They care too much about him.

Ms. Santos is much safer. She has the distance from Dave's decisions that helps her to stay balanced, yet Dave will have access to her all year in social studies class and can see her around the school after that. She takes the time to listen, sympathizes with a real dilemma, and, in this case, knows something about what other countries are like. She makes Dave feel as if he is being a thoughtful person and not just a bratty teenager lashing out at what is frustrating him. The respect she shows him in class—putting off the day's schedule—sends a powerful signal of acceptance. She takes him seriously, helping him to identify and then weigh his choices. Without sermons, with only a few artfully posed questions and the promise to return to the discussion whenever Dave wants, she exhibits the kind and rational behavior which is especially important to teenagers who are beginning to consider adult lives. She is *modeling* a certain way to approach knotty problems.

AS INDIVIDUALS, the Ms. Santoses can model. So too can a school, by its collective signals and its tangible priorities, "model" what is worthy and what is not.

Many Americans are familiar with the Westinghouse high school science prize winners who smile shyly at us each year from the safety of the newspaper photographs. The winners and other finalists from, say, a science-oriented magnet school in New York City, are usually bunched informally by the photographer, all happily dazed by their good fortune and the attention being placed upon it. At their side is their teacher, smiling too.

The article about the winners usually quotes the young people, and their teacher is asked about them. "Yes, these are great kids. They worked very hard. They deserve the best . . ." The students respond in kind. "Mr. Jones helped us so much. . . . He was in the lab with us all the way."

What is it that makes some students hurl themselves at an academic challenge, overcome false starts, keep going, and bring the task to a good conclusion?

Much is involved. None of it is impossible in some form at virtually every school, if its leaders insist on and protect it.

There must be a challenge, a clear target that is perceived as worthy both by the adolescents and by the larger society. Westinghouse, or its counterparts, have to be out there, providing the tingle of competition. The competition has to be authentic, the presentation of a sophisticated answer to a real and demonstrably important question. Can I answer my question better than all the other brainy kids can answer theirs? The intellectually feisty kids wonder. Sure I can.

The work is theirs, not an exercise assigned by someone else, a teacher, testmaker, or curriculum planner. It is science, but it is the science that emerges from their own interests. It is *their* science. The tonic of that ownership is palpable, recognized as each winner talks with reporters. It is *my* project, *our* project.

There are tolerant parents, interested parents, expectant parents, encouraging parents—or surrogate parents, an aunt, a mentor, a neighbor. Yes, they say, you can work on your project all weekend and, no, you need not take a paying job this winter. Yes, you can leave the mess from your research here. How are you getting on? Let me see what you have in mind. Can I help? You must do this. It is exciting. It is good for you. It will help you get a scholarship to Cal Tech.

There is a knot of like-minded kids, youngsters for whom the ascent into the struggle with an academic abstraction is a special joy and who will not mock anyone who dares to make that ascent. That is, there is a gang of what others may derisively (or jealously) call nerds who provide a sanctuary of sufficient size to give comfort and protection.

There is a safe place to work, such as a garage or the corner of a laboratory in a classroom and the rudiments of equipment to get started. There is time to work, before and after school. No janitor keeps you out on the street until 7:15 A.M. and makes you leave at 4:15. Indeed, the janitor loiters briefly some of the days, to find out about your work and give his encouragement.

There is a school that cares about what you are doing and a teacher, a Mr. Jones or Ms. Cho, who nurtures you, getting you thinking about the prospect when you are a tenth grader, joshing you into a particular scientific interest not only in class but outside of class, chiding you when you slacken, making sure that you have the academic tools to do a piece of serious science, showing you about doing science by doing it himself or herself.

And, surely, there is a *je ne sais quoi* quality found in such adolescents, a spark that ignites both curiosity and the stubborn ingenuity to pursue the answers to arresting questions. Whether one is born with such a spark or captures it from experience is too elusive a question to answer, but the context in which a young person lives and studies—that youngster's school—surely and powerfully counts. Some schools and families produce genuinely questing students. Some do not.

THE CONDITIONS that nurtured Dave and the science whizzes are not particular to schoolkeeping. Milbrey McLaughlin and her colleagues looked carefully at what they called "urban sanctuaries," neighborhood organizations that attracted and served inner-city youth, especially those who were drifting, at odds with society. Those that succeeded, in the sense that the adolescent participants found constructive meaning and sensible direction from activities there, were places that had "family-like environments in which individuals are valued and rules of membership are clear. Their activities offer oppor-

tunities for active participation and present challenges that result in accomplishments as defined by youth as well as the larger
society. . . . They are youth driven and sensitive to youth's ev-
eryday realities. . . . They assume that youth are a resource to
be developed, not a problem to be solved. They are flexible . . .
tangibly local . . . They enable youth through family-like challenging, prodding, nagging, teasing, loving."

These "urban sanctuaries" are in many respects similar in
their functioning and in the attitudes they foster to those available within the schoolhouse. The "sanctuaries," the science
teams and the social studies classes are small, made up of
groups of young people and one or a few adults who have the
chance to know and support each other. They have goals,
whether quite specific, such as a science prize, or more diffuse,
such as the creation of a safe and rewarding place where important matters can be discussed. They have rules, usually crafted
by their participants, but congruent with the best of those of
the larger society. They are voluntary; the participants are
sought after, but they have to buy in.

They are intense; they do not function with casual participation. The work of each has a reward, either obvious (a prize)
or subtle (association with a group of trusted friends). They
are respectful of the power, however latent, of their adolescent
participants to accomplish worthy work of their own devis-
ing. They are safe, physically and psychologically. They have
adult leaders who act as mentors or coaches—as friends—rather
than only as dispensers of information. The teenagers are surrounded by people who make the prospect of taking charge of
one's own head and heart possible.

These are the values that ought to permeate high school. Institutions, large and small, which are organized around the
principle of helping adolescents to grow sturdily into adult-

hood can be places which model goodness. Furthermore, evidence of goodness need not be limited to behavior; it can also be found in the thoughtful choice of one argument over another or even in the most private stirrings of the heart, stirrings which are only glimpsed in a dramatic performance or a line in a student's poetry. The three groups described above—two inside schools, one outside—are creating a context for moral growth.

These groups have countless counterparts, the most familiar in schools being sports teams, newspaper editorial boards, drama companies, and academic "teams" such as those preparing to compete for an Odyssey of the Mind prize. Adults operate similarly. Students in law schools create study groups and mock trial teams. Art and architecture schools provide cavernous studios where students usually work at close quarters in what is structured and enormously productive chaos. Most large churches and synagogues are the sum of all sorts of gathered smaller communities, committees, planning and service groups, workshops, governing boards. The military emphasizes the collective commitments of small groups of men and women—gun crews, rifle squads and platoons, teams of Navy Seals, most of them made up of people in their late teens. Most successful politicians and managers have their inner, honest and reinforcing groups. And it is not for nothing that celebrated criminals are usually part of what the public calls "gangs." Humans are animals who gather.

Why and how and whether they gather makes a difference. Context counts. The way a place or group is arranged, the nature of the incentives for that group to do whatever seems most important to do (for good or ill) and the quality of the human interactions are pivotal. The context teaches by how it is structured and how the participants interact.

The contexts can be intentional. Ms. Santos's class certainly is, and so are those created for students hooked on science or for city adolescents attracted to a group which promises constructive safety. Or they can be antisocial, a gathering of people for their own protection and efficiency, for example in the traffic of illegal drugs. Or the contexts can be the product of mindlessness, places and situations that emerge from a long-forgotten necessity but exist now without plan or reason. Or they can be constructed primarily for the administrative convenience of people, often dismissed contemptuously as "bureaucrats," who labor far away from the group. Or they may be merely the happenstance sum of actions and policies devised for different purposes. That is, they may be unintentional communities.

High schools are one of America's most ubiquitous intentional communities. They exist to prepare youth for the adult world. Most American adolescents are required to go to school, and they attend schools which enroll a thousand or more pupils. Most high schools are organized to manage the flow of these diverse pupils over a series of carefully described activities with the least possible hassle at the least possible cost. Though high schools were originally designed with the sorts of values implicit in the examples we have cited, demands for order and efficiency have long commandeered the priorities of the architects of American secondary schools.

More is the pity. By means of their design, all high schools teach. Their rules and routines are lessons of substance and value. Thoughtfully or unthinkingly, students and teachers ingest these values, thereby learning to live by them. These lessons may promote optimism or cynicism, hard work or shortcuts. Most often, because so many schools have become unintentional communities—that is, have strayed from their original purposes—they promote different attitudes in different classes, so that the student herself is left with the job of sorting it all out. Furthermore, while high school is but part of an adolescent's life, it is an influential one. The quality of that experience leaves its mark.

H IGH SCHOOLS have long had three core tasks: to prepare young people for the world of work; to prepare them to use their minds well, to think deeply and in an informed way; and to prepare them to be thoughtful citizens and decent human beings.

While a typical high school attempts to be true to these ends, in practice, even when undertaken by decent and devoted people, it often falters. Most high schools are friendly and, for most students, safe places, and most prepare their students moderately well for college and work.

Few, however, are organized to encourage the relationship between students and their teachers such as that between Dave and Ms. Santos. The loads per teacher are normally heavy—100 to 175 young people during each semester—and the rapid reassignment of students from course to course makes it likely that a large percentage of students are not known well. This creates a situation which is, unfortunately, welcomed by many students: anonymity means their freedom from all sorts of scrutiny and obligation.

The formation of "thoughtful citizens and decent human beings" is, of the three, the oldest and most controversial of high schools' traditional tasks. The goal itself raises all sorts of questions. What kind of people does our community desire and deserve? How might the young people's values be shaped? Do public schools have the right to "shape" a student's mind, or was Bartlett Giamatti correct when he said that such an invasion of the "contours of another person's mind . . . would be an act of terrorism"?

High schools are surrounded by these questions, questions as good as they are ancient. As a practical matter high schools have to reduce them to a number which is both feasible and essential. What do we stand for in this place? How is that stance reflected in our routines, activities, and rituals? How do we *model*—as institutions and as the people who work within them—that which we most value?

The kids count on our consistency. Few qualities in adults annoy adolescents more than hypocrisy. Familiar examples abound. The English teacher who insists that her students read fiction but who never reads any herself. The social studies teacher who neither knows who the candidates are in a local election nor bothers to vote. The physical education teacher who is, whatever his or her age, grossly out of shape. The assistant principal who acts on the basis that a student is guilty until proven innocent, even as he teaches the opposite in his ninth-grade social studies class. The principal who lectures his students about fairness but who coddles the children of influential families.

There are also positive examples that tell their own story. The biology teacher who, spring after spring, tracks the nesting patterns of red-winged blackbirds, dragging his students before dawn into a mosquito-infested swamp to watch and record the movements of the birds. The English teacher who writes poetry, shares it with her students, and not only teaches drama but directs student performances. The coach who keeps on top of her game, razor-sharp on new rules, plays, and practices and always ready to share them. The custodian who in his work exhibits pride of place and insistently, politely, and persuasively expects the students to do likewise. The assistant principal who makes certain he learns the name of every student within a month of the opening of school and who greets and treats each student with knowing familiarity. The teacher who organizes a "coffeehouse" every month where people of all ages present poems, songs, dances, duets, skits, short essays. All these people bear witness to values many feel are the province of a public school.

The people in a school construct its values by the way they address its challenges in ordinary and extraordinary times. Again, familiar examples display the lessons which adults may *not* wish to be teaching: toleration of endemic cheating by a faculty which has run out of energy and, thus, strategies; favoritism shown to athletes, who get easy assignments in class and whose out-of-school high jinks are tolerated; mockery of kids who work hard at activities sponsored by the school; suspicion and mistrust demonstrated by the security officer, festooned with a radio apparatus, patrolling a corner in a hallway, challenging kids as they hove into view. The kids laugh about him and his schtick, mock him behind his back, but they learn from his distrustful stance what their school thinks of them. They think we are dirt, they tell us.

There are happier examples, also known to us. The empathetic courtesy at a school assembly given to a long-winded visiting speaker or to a fellow student who forgets his lines or sings flat. Generous recognition by the crowds in the stands to a valued player on an opposing team who is injured during a close game. The use of the school as a place in which to introduce some of its seventeen-year-olds to the practice of giving blood. Gathering crews of teenaged snow shovelers to be put at the service of the town police during a major, crippling snowstorm to dig out both the entrances to essential public services and the homes of housebound elderly. Closing school (even in technical violation of a school system rule) to attend the funeral of a student who was killed in a freak automobile accident in full view of many students.

Institutions can bear witness, in good and bad times. That is, they can *model* certain kinds of behavior.

The persistent question is, of course, *which* behaviors, *which* values, *which* qualities are to be modeled. Lists of such virtues have been made and argued about for centuries; no topic in the history of education has attracted so much analysis and attention. The possibility of original sin in the young, or the unrepressed irresponsibility of the adolescent, or the cruel prejudices of adults controlling the schools have vexed generations of Americans.

Samuel Phillips in 1778 tied morals and learning together in a classic knot, instructing the Master (the one-man faculty) of the academy bearing his name as follows: "above all, it is expected, that the Master's attention to the disposition of the *Minds* and *Morals* of the Youth, under his charge, will exceed every other care; well considering that, though goodness without knowledge (as it respects others) is weak and feeble; yet knowledge without goodness is dangerous; and that both united form the noblest character, and lay the surest foundation of usefulness to mankind."

At the heart of this expression is an important and persistent American assumption that "good character" and "morality" are tied to the use of the mind; and that the mind is best used for worthy, indeed moral, ends. Church and state are to be separated for doctrinal purposes, but the inculcation of civil behavior—sometimes even called a civil religion—is a proper task for the public schools.

Many schools wrestle hard with what all of this practically means.

Some reduce it to an enumeration of desirable—but mostly undesirable—behaviors. No cheating. No fighting. No littering. No rudeness. No raucousness.

Some recount the expression of virtues: "You accept things you cannot control with humor and grace; you are tolerant of a delay or confusion or other uncomfortable conditions. You are patient with others. You resolve your conflicts peacefully; you seek a resolution that is fair and just for all." The students and faculty regularly discuss these "criteria for excellence" and the criteria serve as the text from which a school's "justice committees" or their counterparts reach decisions on penalties for alleged miscreants.

Yet others design "contracts" that the school makes with each student, a statement of what goes and what doesn't go in classrooms and hallways and what might happen if a student (or, sometimes, the school) strays from what is expressly and clearly agreed upon.

All three of these approaches inevitably provoke questions and unwittingly disconnect issues of value (and the behavior that flows from them) from the habit of seriously thinking about important matters. That is, matters of value are treated as if they were extracurricular, implying that the intellectual rigor expected, say in calculus class, is not expected in matters of moral concern.

Yet, save for extreme matters such as blatant and premeditated violence in a hallway, for example, most presumed errors of behavior are subject to disagreement. They therefore require a mind which is capable of making distinctions. When is a sort-of copied social studies essay deliberate plagiarism and when is it merely the naive stumble of a fledgling scholar who does not fully understand how to cite another's work? When is a shout of warning in a hallway unwarranted noisiness and when is it a legitimate act to prevent an accident? When might "fighting back" be justified? There are no satisfactory universal and easy answers to any of these questions. All are to some important extent rooted in a particular situation. Only by examining the principle that was apparently violated against the evidence of the offense is there the possibility of reaching a satisfactory conclusion. That is, all the people involved have to *think* about the issue, both in the abstract and with regard to the immediate details.

After over two hundred years, Samuel Phillips is still right: the moral and the intellectual are inextricable. One school turned this complexity into a virtue by creating a system that required careful thought about every appearance of a possibly uncivil act. Charles Merrill, in designing his independent Commonwealth School in Boston some decades ago, posited one rule: *Don't Rollerskate in the Hallways.* Pondered carefully, stretched this way and that, such a dictum served the school as a metaphor for how people should behave. The first expectation in an intentional community is consideration for one's fellow beings. All other mores and rules must follow from that. An incivility was not merely plucked from a list of school "don'ts." It had to find its own place against what appeared to be a whimsical requirement but in fact provided a framework for all kinds of issues. People of all ages had to *think* about their actions, personal and collective.

The modeling of scholarship, such as the tracking of red-winged blackbirds by students and teacher, and the modeling of "behavior," such as living what you preach, are of the same substance. Rarely are they treated so in schools. The large American high school which was originally meant to promote careful thinking among all of the people has become a monument to mindlessness, at least as far as personal conduct is concerned. "Good behavior" is something that applies to students. Adults have no comparable "contract," save a usually ill-defined professionalism. Teachers have no moral equivalent of the Hippocratic oath. Adults can be cruel to others in the students' hearing, without penalty or remorse. Adults do not have to practice the disciplines they teach; indeed, some feel little need even to show enthusiasm for what they teach. The subjects of the curriculum are academic castor oil which students must ingest because it is good for them. For students in such a place, a school's "rules" are usually perceived as strictures that implicitly insist Do what we say, not necessarily what we do—hardly desirable models for a principled life.

But the examples we have cited—a teacher's serious consideration of adolescent questioning, involvement in a science project, and the functioning of "urban sanctuaries"—suggest the possibility of a different arrangement.

The "rules" in Ms. Santos's classroom are those of consideration for another's dilemma and of reasonable and confident problem-solving. The "rules" of evidence in serious science are demanding, and the prospect of defending one's project before judges whom you have never met is threatening. One *has* to get it right. The "rules" and customs of a community which is a legitimate "sanctuary" are in their classification by the participants and in their application no less demanding. One *has* to get them right.

In each case, the "rules" apply to all involved, not only the students. Young and old create thoughtful communities, fashion or borrow their "rules," and function by and within them. The ways that each community pursues its work are rational, devised by human minds, and principled in that they provide a framework for fair, safe, honest, and decent conduct. The minds and morals of every person involved are engaged. None is exempt. There is little hypocrisy to be found here.

INDIVIDUALS ARE one thing. The school as a whole—the institution—is another. Desirable ends cannot be wholly limited to the individual or even to the small pockets of civility and purpose which we have described, and which can be found in nearly every school. They apply deeply to the community as a whole.

Amitai Etzioni puts it usefully. "The basic social virtues are a voluntary moral order and a strong measure of bounded individual and subgroup autonomy, held in careful equilibrium." Schools have to have a collective culture, a "moral order," but one which is in balance with individual autonomy.

Two words are of special importance. The moral order is *voluntary*; the adults and the students are partners in its creation and maintenance. Both students and teachers see the point of schooling. In small and voluntary associations, shared norms emerge which make it unnecessary to devise elaborate sets of rules. The rules that last come out of environments, not books. The relationship between the needs of the community and individual freedom is not something arbitrarily imposed; it is, rather, arrived at through explanation, exploration, and persuasion.

In a school, this is difficult to do. Younger students have little experience in this process and often are impatient with it to the point of intolerance. "They need structure," it is explained, "and clarity." Adults, who will be held ultimately responsible, often feel outnumbered, put in corners by youth and often by their well-organized adult special interest "spokesmen."

There is strain in all of this, but the end does justify the means. A community's functioning rests on trust, and trust comes from the understanding that emerges from dialogue. Such is a justifiable cost of democracy, even among unequals, such as those within schools which are gathered for the older (the more powerful) to teach the younger.

The second critical word is *equilibrium*. There has to be a unified (if not precisely uniform) culture. And there has to be room for the appropriate expression of individual convictions.

These two are not necessarily in opposition, but they can be. Among a few very important things, school is about helping young people to gain the habit of seeing the virtue of such a balance, not only at school but in all the years that follow. One is true to oneself. One is also true to one's communities. Each citizen must find his or her most defensible balance. School exists to help along that process.

A LL OF this is not to suggest that there is no struggle. The great human questions persist. What is moral? What is civilized? What is good character? The answers are neither easy nor likely to be readily settled. Schools are necessarily afloat in a soup of ambiguity, one which is accompanied by strong feeling and, often, paralyzing confrontation.

To find the core of a school, don't look at its rulebook or even its mission statement. Look at the way the people in it spend their time—how they relate to each other, how they tangle with ideas. Look for the contradictions between words and practice, with the fewer the better. Try to estimate the frequency and the honesty of its deliberations. Though it will always want to spruce up for visitors, its hour by hour functioning is what is important. Judge the school not on what it says but on how it keeps.

2 *Grappling*

S C H O O L is a frustration for Carl, because he can't see the good it does him. Even more, he can't see the good he does *it*. In social studies, the teacher tells him which American presidents were the greatest. At least she also tells him exactly why—his parents say he should be grateful for that; they only got to memorize the list, never to hear the explanations—so it's interesting to think about. Still, he'd like to have the chance to tell her why he thinks a president who manages to avoid a war is as good as one who leads a nation in a war.

In math, he's told that there is one right answer and one way to get to that right answer. In English, he's told that the music lyrics on which he dotes are inferior poetry. Even when he is asked to write, he's told how many paragraphs he should use to get his ideas across to "the" reader. Which reader? Wouldn't it matter who she was?

And when his teacher takes his class down to the computer room, to find a substitute there who doesn't know how to run the new machines, he's not allowed to read the computer manual so that he can help to get the class started. He tries to argue that he's done this before, at home and even at school, and that the class needs the time in the lab if they are to finish their projects. But he gets a little too near to rudeness, and the teacher, visibly upset, cuts him off. "I don't know what's happened to the kids these days," she says to us as she turns the class around to wait out the period in her room. "They're so irresponsible."

In fact, this situation requires deeper consideration. There is, of course, no guarantee that Carl could have figured out how to run the new machines and thus saved the time for his classmates and his teacher. It's hard to predict how much time his grappling would have taken, or what its outcome would have been. The problem could have been "solved" on a superficial level or it might have needed a lot more work. Carl's energy might have given out; he might even have hurt the equipment. Nor is there an excuse for the rudeness that those who know more than others about technology—or other subjects—often display.

Still, all day Carl was treated as if he were an empty vessel, as if his skills and his opinions were of no value to those around him. In the computer room, he was told that there was nothing which he or anyone else could do to fill that vessel up. Instead, they were to go back to their classroom and act as if they weren't there. The result was an intellectual and a moral vacuum.

Why does an intellectual vacuum so often lead to a moral one as well? Schools exist for children, but children are often seen as the school's clients, as its powerless people. They are told that they are in school not because of what they know but because of what they don't know. All over the world, powerless people lose the instinct to help, because it is so often rebuffed in them. Yet, even if he had eventually been unsuccessful, struggling with the computer manual would have been a good use of Carl's mind. He would have been fulfilling the real purpose of schooling: to equip himself to be of use. He would have used what he already knew to reach out and learn more about how computers work. And he would have put himself on the line in a good cause.

PUTTING ONESELF on the line may be preferable, but it invites the kind of criticism which is rarely applied to the young. Raising them is an exquisitely tricky business. A fiftyish father grumped to us about his daughter, just graduating from high school. The young woman had announced to her parents that she was determined to become a writer. "A writer?" Dad snorted to us. "What would she write about? She doesn't *know* anything."

The young woman was full of passion. She liked to string words out, playing with them. She wrote exclusively about her own world, casting it as revelation. She labored hard in English courses and had several intense pieces published in the school's literary magazine. She had skimmed over her other courses, doing only the minimum. Nonetheless, she was an honors student. She surely would get a book award at graduation, deservedly so.

And yet Dad had a telling point. Behind his daughter's enthusiasms was glibness. Her skill was admirable, and her joy in the application of that skill was palpable. Her ability to describe her own thoughts and feelings was unusual. But the young woman did not even know that she knew relatively little, that there was important knowledge that required a broader context than her own life.

The father, caught in the practical demands of earning a living, tired of years of teenaged hubris, is understandably cautious. But if he is smart, he will keep his concerns to himself. The energy, even the presumption, of the young writer should not be reined in just because so much of it is based on self-absorption and naiveté. Instead, in taking herself seriously and wanting to write for an ever-widening audience she will be motivated to take an increased interest in the ways of the world. Time will tell.

This is how we have seen growing up work, in case after case.

A student's hope and sense of agency is often dependent on her sense that there is something she can do which is valued by others. Not just other kids, but adults as well. And not empty "self-esteem-building activities," but the outcome of her best efforts, in which she has real confidence. From that point on, talent intertwines constantly with content, as the student challenges herself to perform at higher levels for a broader audience.

A ND S O it is with learning the habits of civil behavior. The skills are important. Showing restraint. Being willing to listen. Empathy. Feeling responsible for something and some people beyond oneself and one's personal coterie of friends. Being nice. Getting along in one's daily interactions.

But there must be more. Most interactions in life are complex; more than talent and good habits are needed to address them well. Few are mastered by merely applying a slogan such as "Just Say No." Context is critical if not crucial. The thoughts and resultant actions of (say) a Polish-German day laborer working near Auschwitz in 1944, a person who sees the full trains come and the empty trains go, might be appreciably different from the conclusions about the Holocaust reached by an outraged American teenager sitting in an unthreatened high school classroom fifty years later. It will help the teenager to absorb complexity if he can reflect from the shoes of the laborer, not necessarily to agree but to empathize, to understand. In this Second World War moment there is powerful stuff: the particulars of a situation, in necessarily exquisite and painful detail. That stuff, if well and carefully considered, provides the perspective which is the heart of ultimately truly moral decisions. Educators call this *content*.

The habits of civil behavior can do much to bring safety to a school's halls. But the meanings of civil behavior are much tougher to present. They transcend one's immediate environment. When fully and painstakingly constructed, they provide a distant mirror, the meaning of one's immediate condition against a sweep of human and environmental experience, past and present.

One has to *grapple* with those meanings. If not, "behavior" is reduced to glib catchwords, ones that provoke little more than periodic puffs of self-righteousness. A curriculum which is rich in content will teach young people that important matters of sensitive living have everything to do with hard, substantive, and often agonizingly painful thought. The students will write plays or stories or imagined memoirs which will help them to get at the considerations inside that hypothetical day laborer's head.

Grappling is necessarily a balancing act. One is trying to do what one has never done before and learning more about what one wants to do. The reader's sense of his own power is built up by letting him try to understand the computer manual so the class can go forward. The writer's humility and appreciation of context is built up by asking her to take on another's complex identity before she tries to write about it. Each task is doable but difficult; each requires that the student put him or herself firmly on the line.

The first step in creating such a demanding curriculum is to believe that it can be done. Wise schoolpeople and parents should not underestimate the power that they can find in young minds, bodies, and hearts. Recently the newspapers reported that an eleven-year-old took her younger cousin on a three-hour drive in the family car, crossing state lines, navigating competently, looking for an uncle but settling for an aunt. Everyone who commented on the incident remarked on how naughty these children were, how neglectful was the mother who had left them and the keys in the car while she went to an exercise salon, how unobservant was the gas station operator who sold them gas without noticing how young they were. No one wondered at the sheer competence lurking like a shadow underneath the youngsters' foolishness.

We're selling our children short when we believe that grappling is beyond them. In fact, most of them are engaging in dilemmas of intense seriousness while we're looking the other way. Most teenagers have watched one or another substance be abused, heard adults who are important to them treat each other harshly, wondered why so many are poor in a rich country. Many have been mugged figuratively, and some even literally. The teenage mother or caregiver has been a fixture for centuries. Most modern wars have been fought (albeit neither started nor led) by teenage males. The Confederates defended Atlanta in 1864 with an army made up of grandfathers and their grandsons. The American paratroopers at D-Day were nineteen-year-olds led by twenty-two-year-old company commanders. The ill-equipped armies in central Africa in the 1990s are full of teenagers.

Whether older folks like it or not, children driving cars should not be perceived as all that exceptional. To treat adolescents as delicate flowers unable to act and think is a costly pretense, as patronizing as it is wasteful. Young people can do things and they do do things, now. Older folk should accept that fact and labor hard to provide the perspective that can affect and inform, in a principled way, the actions that young people, willy nilly, will take.

Adolescents are no different from the rest of us. They resist mandates issued from on high, and most of them won't be forced into good habits, but they are willing to talk about moral choices and they can decide that some courses of action are better than others. In fact, they are eager to come to opinions on these matters, as long as they are trusted to take their time and examine their assumptions as carefully as they can. They can do this in school by considering example after example—some literary, some historical, some scientific—which are interesting and nuanced and in which a human must decide between possible actions. When they work it all through in a variety of assignments, they learn much about literature and history and the human condition. All of this considering is what helps the teenager to develop his or her own moral code. This last and most private step in the process is the most important one. Finally, the test of a good school is how its students behave when no one is looking, how they are in the mall as well as in the school's classrooms and corridors.

A central vehicle for this teaching is the school's formal curriculum. There are matters of deep value embedded in all sorts of traditional classes, in the sciences as well as the humanities and the arts. Wise schools use these places for grappling, not only for matters normally expected in (say) a science or history class but also for occasions to deepen each student's habit of confronting, and thus deepening, his or her understanding of values.

Most teachers are fond of the word "engagement," because it means that the students are really taking an interest in the work which the teacher has designed for them. Grappling, however, goes one step further. It presumes that the student has something to add to the story. Either hypothetically or actually, the student is asked to join the struggle, to add his or her input.

The input may be in the form of added information. High school students who are analyzing the racial and ethnic disagreements in their city may be asked to research immigration patterns, previous political relationships, or a number of other factors to get a clearer picture of what is in the minds of those who are involved in contemporary problems. The information students collect can be scrutinized carefully by their classmates, their teacher and outside groups, both for the way it was gathered and for what it means. If it was gathered in the traditional ways of research, it can reinforce those habits, which are basically good ones: honesty, freedom from bias, orderly procedures, and so forth. If it was gathered in unconventional ways, such as through chats with one's highly prejudiced uncle, those ways can be analysed and even justified, at least on certain grounds. Once gathered, the research can be presented in graphs and photographs, essays and statistics, with much discussion of the way each format will be able to contribute to an overall understanding of the situation.

The students' input may also be in the form of opinion. Most high school students spend much time considering such matters as pushing and shoving—or even more violent activities—and whether they are dangerous or are an inevitable part of life. They think about deterrence: when and how much a threatened punishment keeps them from doing something. They think about authority, and what its best and worst uses ought to be. They think about ethnicity and how much it influences a person's overall approach to things. They question the religion which has been important to their family, the grandmother who believes that they ought to write thank-you notes, the teacher who takes offense at sloppy work. They are at an unsettled time in life when their many different ideas and observations are starting to form themselves into opinions which they may keep all their lives.

We should be grateful for their confusion: it is part of life to think for oneself, and nature needs that little blip between generations. We can learn to live with and even harness (though that may be a "bad word," a "restrictive" concept) the teenagers' energy by learning to take advantage of it. The thoughts which are roiling around in the students' heads should be invited out and put to work. They should be applied to schoolwork, the better to develop and grow in the sunlight, the better to be made subject to others' questions. Schoolwork is about violence and deterrence and authority and tradition and behavior. We should invite the students' input into the subject of whether the Civil War could have been avoided, of whether the southern states' desire to secede from the Union was legitimate self-determination or a dangerous threat to the very concept of democracy. Schoolyard tension and even family regroupings are not precisely analogous to the Civil War, of course. But the students' opinions will be refined and strengthened, not by avoiding such analogies, but by pressing to make them more accurate and appropriate.

Finally, we can cultivate but also acknowledge the students' skills. Why should the local malls be the only ones who know how to appreciate responsible teenagers? Besides the ability to do research, they have mathematical, artistic, writing, and speaking skills which can be valued in a complex world. Many high schools have peer mediation programs now, and students are learning much about identifying others' needs and interests and finding a common ground between them. These skills can be applied to a wider arena: at first in hypothetical role plays and under close supervision, but later with a somewhat more autonomous structure and in real situations, such as student-run businesses which raise money for the poor.

TEXT-BASED discussions are also amenable to grappling. For all sorts of reasons, many contemporary high school students read Harper Lee's *To Kill a Mockingbird*, a story of race, guilt, innocence, and courage set in the American South in the 1930s. The story displays the importance of evidence and argument. It exhibits raw courage and the toughness of honesty. In our times, it is the sort of tale which usually provokes moral outrage and, with that outrage, the attention and engagement of high school students.

How could people so blatantly discriminate against black people and their white defenders? The question is a good one, but perhaps one particular to who we are today. Did Americans respond to Lee's story in previous decades with similar moral outrage? If not, why not? Are we all slaves to the received mores of our own times? And why did Lee choose this story? Was it her intention to present a morality tale? Are such tales in themselves vehicles for stressing a particular set of values for all their readers? If so, should such tales be told in public schools?

Lee's story clearly describes a polarized community. Why did folks in Finch's Landing so fear one another? Why, every day everywhere, do folks find others threatening? Does the threat of one time and place find its counterpart in other times and places; or was *Mockingbird* a tale of one peculiar and particular place and time? If so, can one ever learn from example?

Why do people "discriminate" in the harsh way described in the book? "Discrimination" in itself is not necessarily pejorative. We learn to admire people who are "discriminating," in the sense that they are skilled in making fine and useful distinctions. Much of serious mathematics is about such distinctions: are there "values" involved here as well, and, if so, what is the nature of these values? Is recognizing differences necessarily a bad thing? If not, when is it tolerable and when is such differentiation harmful?

The litany of good questions is endless. To ponder them is to grapple—or even wrestle—with specific and carefully described ideas that are freighted with values. A student who grapples is made aware of this complexity; and if there is an explicit expectation by the school and its teachers that this sort of grappling is as worthy as it is complex, the student may get into the habit of the struggle, a struggle more important than its ultimate resolution. The teacher must really be interested, however, in what the students' "answers" are. If they are shallow, if they are biased, the teacher needs to help the students to develop them further but not necessarily to replace them neatly with the teacher's own conclusions.

Fiction is particularly useful in this kind of discussion, because it gets the student outside of herself. It provides a new and unfamiliar setting to play out enduring issues and thus avoids the pressures of the immediate or personal. The sense of suspense in the narrative draws in even those students who do not feel comfortable in moral discussions.

Teachers can catch the heat that arises from a careful discussion of issues such as those raised by *To Kill a Mockingbird* and use it to deepen the talk, to broaden the questions, and to demand that the students use the text to support their arguments. Circling back over familiar ground, asking new sorts of questions about that ground, looking for every scrap of data, are necessary steps in building the habit of thoughtful grappling.

In a lively class, the time will come to leap beyond the text to confront in the abstract the issues raised by the narrative. Since the question of justice winds through the novel, an attempt to define the abstraction "justice" can now emerge. And then there may be further discussion of what and how it means to live in a community which harbors varied meanings of the word *justice*. And still more discussion about how to address the practical expressions of those meanings. How can fairness be offered to young and old, black and white, assured and fearful, gregarious and reclusive, all in the same community?

Generously pursued, such classroom conversations stick in the students' minds. They will think about discriminations good and bad; they will grapple with what they find to be persuasively "good" or "bad" in this context; and they will have been exposed to the issues of discrimination and justice, ones of fundamental importance in a democracy.

The students may sense the teacher's personal views and be greatly influenced by them. However, they will also see that issues of this weight are complex, that interpretations differ among thoughtful, decent people. Few issues of value can be reduced to sharply painted absolutes. Exceptions are made even to the dictum "thou shall not kill," for example, by many in the armed services or those in the criminal justice system charged with carrying out legal executions. Depending on one's viewpoint on when life begins, a question of the definition, and therefore the value, of life may arise over the issue of abortion. There are few easy answers to central moral concerns for Americans. This is why young people must be given practice in grappling with them in as informed and principled a manner as possible.

There are dangers in all this. Students may find stories such as *To Kill a Mockingbird* too depressing, or feel that their teachers are excessively eager to expose the serious issues underlying texts. They may find the attempt to teach toward a habit of thoughtfulness about issues of value contrived, humorless, and, at worst, intrusive. But for many students, insisting that they tackle important and demonstrably relevant ideas such as the meaning of justice is a tonic. It is one very important reason to be in school. They want more.

When the students stick to a text such as *Mockingbird* long enough to understand the abstractions in it, they are likely to apply that understanding to the next text. *Othello. Schindler's List.* The Sacco and Vanzetti case from the 1920s. Why is the "different" person so often distrusted? Is there a clear line between American nativism, as expressed by the Sacco-Vanzetti trial, and the Nazi ferocity depicted in Spielberg's movie? Is this pattern of fear and discrimination a modern phenomenon? What of Shakespeare's Moor, Othello? What of Jesus, the Jew and Messiah? What of us today, in our school?

A novel can thus lead a class into many places, with the depth of study growing as the interest deepens. Careful grappling is its own reward; it leads to further grappling. The result is not only a sense of the complexity of moral judgments but also an understanding of the nature of creativity and of scholarship.

Literature is but one field which can provide the stuff, or the point of departure, for thinking deeply about ethical matters such as justice. History itself is stories. Fact and fiction can both be the grist for moral discussions.

When studying the New Deal a teacher can provide students chapters from several well-known but ideologically varied social studies texts of the 1940s and ask them to explain from these texts' "stories" what the New Deal was, what it accomplished and what it meant. How was the New Deal an expression of some fundamental ideas about the obligations of the state in relationship to the obligations and needs of the people? Students are likely quickly to find their favorite texts. The teacher can then push back, asking the students to defend the "story" as told there. Does the text presume certain aspects of human nature or of the economy or of the government which are similar to the student's own opinions? In which respects are the text's arguments supported by the particular facts which are gathered in it? In which respects are they persuasive due to widely accepted social science "data"? How does such data and the interpretations which arise from it come to be "widely accepted," and how do such interpretations change over time? How do historians reach a verdict on how well a president such as Franklin Roosevelt has done? How do these verdicts change over time? The resulting debate—likely to be controversial—can drive students to more data, deeper and deeper, and to a wonderment about just what is historical "truth."

Is there life on Mars? If we don't know, how might we define "life" so that we know what we are looking for? Is there a strictly defensible and sharp divide between inert and living matter? Can this be scientifically determined? If not, what might this mean? How can answers to such questions survive systematic logical and observed analysis? If they can't, what compromises are possible to make and still retain a defensible definition of "proof"? Are there substances in our neighborhood which live on the line between organic and inert matter, and can we examine them? What can we find out about them? And can that inquiry assist us in answering questions about how to ascertain the likelihood of life on Mars?

Was mathematics discovered or invented? Does the answer make any difference for how we might study or depend on that discipline? We talk of "proof," but when is our assurance absolute? If it isn't, how then do we proceed? Is there another word which we might use? Might the architecture of mathematics be applied to other fields, its logic to that of morals, for example?

What is zero? If you can multiply by zero, is there ever nothing? The philosophy of mathematics arises easily from its simplest uses. It raises issues no less complex and important than those of justice and the nature of life.

The deeper a person of whatever age gets into a topic or discipline, the more likely is she to want to dig deeper. The difference between grappling and other forms of learning is that when the questions become the student's own, so do the answers. Thus does a birdfeeder outside the kitchen window lure young children to identify birds ("Daddy, a chickadee!") and to wonder why there are so many different kinds outside the window ("Daddy, why do we have crows and nuthatches and downy woodpeckers all eating out of our feeder, and not only chickadees?"), and finally to discover the fact that most of the earth's birds are found elsewhere ("Daddy, why are there so many kinds of birds not at our feeder, and are more being made every day?"). The more the child learns, the more he may want to learn. And most of what is learned—even the identifying markings of winter birds—carries issues of value. Why is this so? Is the cruelty of the hawk "fair"? ("Daddy, are we like hawks?")

Are we like hawks? Digging deep—grappling—is a reality check. What is the evidence that this is so? How can it be defined? Is it like other things or ideas? Does it connect with matters we already understand? Is it real? Does it matter? If it matters, how am I affected? And finally, most importantly, how should I respond or behave?

UNFORTUNATELY, the sort of grappling described here is all too rare in American high schools. Few teachers have been given the support and incentives to gain a deep grasp of their subjects. Knowledge and authority on the teacher's part are usually required to teach in the interrogatory manner that will provoke the students to grapple. The larger the question, the more likely that the students will grow frustrated, at least at first. Only a confident coach can help his students to move through that frustration to a greater clarity. It is much easier to give a lecture on the three causes of the French Revolution than to question the nature of revolution itself. The conventional educational metaphor is one of delivery, not of constructive, generative provocation. To teach grappling, teachers have to model it, which is difficult to do in a typical high school.

There are other factors as well. Given the sweeping nature of high school curricula—a bit of this and much of that, Cleopatra

to Clinton, the history of China in two weeks, all branches of
biology in a year—few schools are able to allow the time necessary to grapple. As long as the end result of high school is
measured in "coverage," and as long as "coverage" is assumed
by testing the student's memory of a subject, there will be no
time for the students' own questions. Inquisitiveness, skepticism, and imagination are rarely priorities in state "curriculum
frameworks" or on all too many standardized tests. The spiral-
ing of ideas, the testing and retesting and testing again of hy-
potheses, the unpredictability of any one class, the messiness
of this kind of inquiry will put the bravest and most effective
teachers' students at a certain kind of short-term risk.

Another factor is deportment. High schools are such
crowded places that certain norms seem only sensible. One is
that people should listen to each other talk, which requires that
only one person talk at a time. Most often, that is the teacher,
toward whom most students give the greatest respect. In many
classrooms, the teacher has to shut a student up in order to open
him up; that is, in order to give him the time to digest what else
is being said, by the teacher or by other students.

In a classroom which puts a premium on developing ideas,
everybody's hand would be up. No matter how pleased a
teacher might be by this level of engagement, by the time it was
any one student's turn to speak, coherence would be lost. Loos-
ening up this structure by working in groups or tolerating a certain amount of chaos would upset a lot of people. Some would
be students who need a certain amount of order and predict-
ability to learn, or who get intimidated by their classmates'
ideas or even their confidence. Other upset people might well
be the folks who walk around the school's halls. Observing
from such a distance, it's hard to tell the difference between
excitement and cheekiness. In this situation, it's the teacher
whose initial convictions about the best kind of learning have

been shaken, or have put him on the line. He might be grappling with finding a new job by next spring.

And finally, many schools are afraid of the political ramifications of any sort of teaching that surfaces matters of value, matters which are often controversial and thus threatening. What if Susanna refuses to go to church on Sunday because she's offended by what she learned about its modern policies or even by abuses in the medieval church? What if Carlos can't sleep because he's upset about a predicted raising of the sun's temperature? What if Derek starts lecturing his parents about their smoking? If students take their educations into their own hearts, if they begin to act according to their new discoveries, the dislocations in their own and their families' lives may well be difficult. The students will inevitably make some mistakes, and the school will be a convenient scapegoat.

Grappling with the tough issues is hard work. No matter how smart they sound, most students are new to this game of dealing with controversy. Recently, we visited a class which was learning about the Bill of Rights by discussing a case that involved downloading pornography, how much privacy a student should expect in school, who should decide what reasonable proof is, who has responsibility for the safety of students, and other issues. One couldn't help but be struck, not just by the students' commitment to the discussion, but also by their skill at handling complex concepts, at looking at the background of the case, at imagining outcomes if the case had been handled differently. One young man had an opinion on nearly every aspect; he was very well spoken and seemed confident and persuasive: definitely a lawyer—and a good one—in the making. At the end of the class, though, he jumped up and, with a big smile, said, "But what do *we* know? We're only children!" He wasn't undercutting the sophistication which he'd demonstrated so convincingly earlier. Indeed, he was adding to it by admitting that he had more that he needed to think about, more he needed to learn. His perspective about his own place in life made it seem even more important to let him begin such discussions in school.

Few people in high schools believe that all young people are both capable of this level of work and ready to do it. Because of this, a self-fulfilling prophecy of disinterest is at work. In matters such as the controversy over a national history curriculum, for example, adults with one perspective argue with adults with another perspective. The questions they argue over are important ones, such as how the experiences of native Americans or African slaves or European immigrants should be presented. All of these adults are honorable people who are trying to portray a complicated legacy in as fair and compelling a way as possible. They are mindful of the students they are teaching, in that they agree that the younger students should have a simpler version of history than the older ones do. Teachers, too, are trying to design their lessons so carefully and to teach them so skillfully that there won't be any chance of misinforming, or unnecessarily hurting, their students. What all these concerned adults may be leaving out, however, is the dimension which each learner has to add to material in order really to know it. There has to be a shred of interest there already for the talented teacher to build on. If the interest is built on a shared racial identity, a shared economic identity, a shared psychological identity (such as seventh graders often feel with the rebellious American colonists struggling to get out from under a "mother country"), so be it. Building on already existing connections seems more important than presenting each unit in exactly the same number of days.

When the external tests are administered, however, the honest grappling which the teacher has encouraged may end up harming her kids. Other teachers have prepared their kids better by sticking to the prescribed curriculum, which "covered" immigration and railroad regulation in the same number of days. However, by emphasizing accuracy—by which they mean the ability to sort through semi-right clues to get to the all-right one on a machine-graded test—to the exclusion of all other aspects of the material, these teachers (and the principals and parents who are flogging them to get the test scores up) are neglecting an important part of the process.

The material which stays in the student's head only until the test will never make it into his outlook. When it is in his outlook—when he thinks, for example, of the losses and gains which immigration brought to those who engaged in it, or when she compares the immigration experience with a recent move which she made—it gains moral importance.

When he has gotten his juices up in some way, he will think about such material out of school, argue about it at the dinner table, take a book about it out of the library, choose it for his next paper. Accuracy will start to matter, but only if it follows engagement, only if he has put himself on the line. Only now will he care if he gets his dates right, or if he finds himself changing his interpretation of something. He has started to grapple with a question of importance to him, and it may well emerge into a lifelong interest and a lifelong habit.

Few schools place a high value on questioning, even though it is the habit which is most likely to lead to consequential scholarship and responsible adulthood. Schools are such crowded places: crowded not only with restless bodies but with parents' dreams for their children. No wonder such emphasis is put on order, but order discourages questioning. Surrounded by the disorderliness of too many children, most teachers find themselves waiting for three o'clock, and for Friday, and for vacation, with a longing bordering on obsession. This makes them think in short-run rather than long-run terms. In that context, questions look messy and even rude. Besides, the students' own questions will take more time to answer than the teachers' questions will, because most teachers' questions can be answered on page 554 of the textbook. Better, most school systems seem to say, to present a watery diet of philosophical or psychologized absolutes as a way to avoid conflict while appearing to attend to students' education in matters of value.

But more and more schoolpeople see it differently. They recognize that the moral is embedded in the intellectual, that thinking hard—grappling—in an informed and careful way is the most likely route to a principled and constructive life. The good person has both passion and restraint, respect for evidence and patience when evidence is not readily at hand.

These matters can be deeply embedded in the full academic curriculum. "Moral" or "character" education is neither a discrete curriculum added as an afterthought nor an unreflective activity such as community "service" which has never been probed for its meaning. It is an intellectual undertaking infusing the entire school. And it is led by adults who *know* things, who themselves are grapplers, with all the work and messiness and confusion that rich content entails.

3 Bluffing

ANGELA is propped against a wall of her bedroom, her hair a tangle, sucking on a pencil, moping about her English homework. Angela has a complaint.

The assignment in the novel last night was way too long. Thirty pages is too much for a sophomore, and it's not as if there's only that for homework. The math homework has to be handed in, there's a quiz most days in Spanish, and the history notes are checked at the beginning of class. I'd be a fool to slip up in biology, because old Jonesey ridicules the kids he doesn't like—and he doesn't like most of the kids!

So, of course, English is left for last.

Angela surveys the outside of the paperback novel in her hand. *The Old Man and the Sea.*

Why did Hitchy assign this stupid book? She's okay as a teacher and I like some of the books she gives us, but this one has been ridiculous. A real waste of my time. I prefer books where more happens . . . So I sit here tonight trying to figure out the little changes way inside this boring character and I fall asleep right here on the floor with the light on and the book open. That's what I will do, and my nice Mom will come in and make me get into bed. I'll act really sleepy.

I'm stuck, though. I can't put it off until tomorrow. I have no time in school when I can read. Sometimes if I sit really still and keep my head down I can read in social studies, but tomorrow I have English third period and history fifth. Periods one and two we have a lab in biology, so I'll be out there at the dissection table, with no place to hide a book on my lap.

Maybe I can get Kevin to tell me what happened. Even he admits that I help him with his math homework a lot. Then I'll just speak early in the class so Hitchy thinks I read it and doesn't call on me again. I know she mostly plays detective in those discussions anyway, and little details in the plot are a quick way for her to tell who's doing the reading. I'll get one of those details in early. This plot, though . . . nothing ever happens!

How can I get to Kevin? Stuck in the lab, I can't use the time between first and second period to talk with him. And goddamn homeroom. Usually I'm glad that Billie makes us be quiet, but just this once I wish she'd let us speak. If not Kevin, maybe someone else.

Angela squirms, twists the pencil some more, stares at the ceiling, sits motionless.

Damn, damn, damn. I hope she doesn't ask who's done the reading. If I admit I haven't, I'll be assigned stuff every single night for at least a week. If I pretend, I'll be in a constant state of panic for the whole period. And I get enough of panic in biology.

Angela slips from slouching to laying flat on the floor, the book discarded to her side.

I guess I'll just sit in the back. I'll look a little weak—I've gotten quite good at that—maybe she'll think I don't feel well. She's kind of a pushover with girls who look like they're having their period. I'll smile at her jokes, nod at a few of the other kids' statements, and hope I get enough out of the class to make some kind of an intelligent statement before it's over.

But the real problem is that thirty pages is too long, and the

book is too boring. How can I possibly do all that's expected of me?
What do adults do when they are stuck in this kind of a bind? I
know they cop out any way they can. They should teach that trick
to us in school rather than asking us to read about old men and
big fish.

F IVE MILES away, Elaine Hitchcock tries to get her ten-
month-old daughter Janey to eat rather than to pitch the
Cheerios all over the floor. The dog keeps racing after the roll-
ing cereal pieces, sometimes crashing into Elaine. Her four-
year-old son Neal, sitting motionless on the floor of the kitchen
with a sandwich in his hand, is glued to the television set.

"Neal. Listen to me. Have you eaten anything yet?"

Silence. Neal mesmerized by a cartoon.

"Janey, eat your food. Don't give it all to the dog. Duchess is
too fat already."

Elaine and her husband Bob have these two children, the
dog, and a bit of the house they occupy (the bank owns most of
it). Each has a job, though only she has much security, including the family's health plan. Bob is an adjunct instructor at
a local college, paid a flat per-course rate and hired only on a
term-to-term basis, depending on enrollment. This term, however, he is also an "acting" dean, filling in for a colleague who is
on leave. That brings in more money but gives Bob little time at
home. There is always some sort of ruckus in a residential hall
to sort out. Tonight it is his turn to feed and bathe the kids, but
there has been an emergency.

Elaine rearranges her workload in her head.

What's up for tomorrow? I promised 11B that I'd get their pa-
pers back. Good grief. Twenty-seven of them, and all tonight. 10C
has just started The Old Man and the Sea. *Do I have last year's*

notes about that? How do I play that discussion? What was the plot, anyway? Was there a plot? Why did I assign the book in the first place?

"Duchess, get lost. Janey, I said eat, not feed the dog!"

11F will be getting their papers to me today. I can get them to talk about the writing. That's a good group. Period seven is the Roosevelt Rapper *kids. The paper is coming together. I might even be able to take a peek at the 11Fs' papers while the kids do the layout.*

Bob arrives quite breathless, hungry, full of talk about to-day's crises. It isn't students this time. It is faculty who spent all their energies complaining about their "hopeless" frosh. Their bitching about how these first-years cannot write replaced their getting on with teaching the new freshmen how to write, or so Bob thinks. The instructors complained about their load of sixty eighteen- to-twenty-five-year-olds. Elaine has heard this before, so many times. She carries 118 students. They are younger than college kids, less selective, forced to be in her classroom, and protected by law from being expelled for failing to do much of anything constructive in her courses. And those college teachers think they have it bad! But she has ceased even cursing about the inequity or the unfairness in the college teachers' judgments.

Bob goes on and on, expecting sympathy. Elaine keeps quiet, smiles, tries to look sympathetic. If they argue, it will put off the kids' baths and bedtimes, and she badly needs to do some work tonight. Her mind is on how soon she can get to the 11F papers. And 10C.

The Old Man and the Sea? I don't have time to find last year's notes. How honest should I be with the kids? I hate it when they try to grease by, but it's not as if I've never taught the book before. I'll just ask them to tell me what they thought about the book so far. If enough of them talk, that will bring the details back into my mind. If I admit to them that I haven't reread the assignment, I'll pay for it. Some of them will decide that if I don't prepare, they don't have to prepare. And, of course, a few of them will tell their parents. It's not a good reputation to have, and anyway, I don't deserve it. So tomorrow, I'll just wing it. I know how.

"Neal. Off with the television. Into bath. Janey, you're next. Bob, your mother called. Duchess, out of my way."

What did I do with my briefcase? I can't find anything!

T HE NEXT day 10C will meet as scheduled, to confront *The Old Man and the Sea.* Elaine will ask what the kids thought about the story. Some will start talking. Elaine will pick up bits and details from them, but carefully, staying close only to those particulars which remind her of the text. Angela will sit quietly, with a wan look on her face. After all her worry, she will gratefully find that she needs to say nothing in class. She makes a point of singing a bright "Good Morning!" to Elaine as she walks out at the end of the period.

Both Angela and Elaine are *bluffing*—misleading others by means of an artful demeanor. Elaine displayed the face of confidence even as she lacked confidence. Angela exhibited politeness, attention, and a vulnerability that would provoke sympathy.

Though what each of them did was premeditated and deliberate, neither one was baldly lying. They were not aggressively claiming to be something which they demonstrably were not. Rather, they were playing a shadowy game of not fully representing their actual situations.

Neither was wholly hypocritical. While they did assume poses to use during the class meeting of 10C, they were prepared—if forced into it—to meet some of the conventions of an English lesson. They were discussing the book, and each was trying to learn—or relearn—from the discussion. Elaine could pick up a few clues about *Old Man* and piece together an acceptable class. It was not the superb class that she wished always to have, but she had learned that preparation on her part did not guarantee a superb class, either.

Elaine was often reminded of her mother's advice about housework: handle emergency situations with "a lick and a promise." For today in 10C, all she could manage was a lick. But she knew she needed to keep the private promise she had made to her students. This class was superficial, but she would somehow find the time to shape it into substance tomorrow. Angela, being younger and not a professional, was less aware of her conscience. What did she "owe" anybody? But either before class or within it, she had picked up a few threads of the story. Now she could spin some observations about them which might be interesting and, if she were lucky, relevant.

Both displayed good manners. They made the best of the poor situation in which they found themselves. They did not turn on others or use them as protection. Elaine, for example, could have pulled a snap quiz on the story, a quiz requiring a period-long essay. Her secret would thereby be secure, but it would have imposed an unanticipated and thoughtless burden on the students. (Of course, she'd have to correct such essays, which would put her still farther behind!) Angela did not disrupt the class, thereby deterring Elaine from getting to the text. By playing quiet, she took a risk, but she also thereby allowed others who were better prepared to have the opportunity to learn.

Bluffing is thus not always an offensive act. Sometimes one pretends in order to make others feel better. Rick, that was a *great* talk you gave in assembly. Mrs. Smith, we will miss your deceased husband terribly. Sally, I feel certain that your writing is improving. Nod sympathetically at Bob, instead of telling him you wish he would cut some corners in his work so you wouldn't have to cut so many in yours. These are the "white lies" which are meant to ease human relationships, the oil in the social machinery which helps to avoid unnecessary abrasion. They are not only innocent; they may actually be good.

But other lies, like Elaine's and Angela's preparation for and behavior in 10C, are more self-serving. At that point they cease being entirely "white," and they are everywhere. Capitalist society depends on bluffing. Elaine Hitchcock's little Neal will see an advertisement on television for what is in fact a flimsy, small plastic car. It is presented on the screen to Neal as if it were roaring down the Indianapolis Speedway. The seller doesn't thereby tell a lie; no one explicitly says that this television representation is what will be delivered in the mail or handed out at the fast-food counter along with a hamburger and a soda. It is merely a come-on, misleading without being baldly untruthful. It is a sort of seller's cosmetic. It makes its face pretty by artificial means.

Bluffing is the heart of the game of poker. One fakes one's true feelings, hoping thereby to mislead one's opponents. The poker strategy lies at the heart of modern commerce. Tell people what they want to hear. Put information about nutrition on the back of Janey's cereal box, even if it's in tiny print and in a form which even Mr. Jones, the biology teacher, could not understand. Offer promises. You can be slim. You can have zest. You can look great. You can really understand. You really can have this powerful car. You can save up to fifty percent. You have never heard of this gizmo, but now that you have, you have to have it. It will change your life.

While it is difficult for many educators to admit it, the line between advertising and a formal education is a fuzzy one. Advertisers teach, showing people things that might improve their lives, things they should buy. Educators teach, showing young people how to employ their minds well and with what to stock those minds. Educators select their ideas and then sell them. In each field, especially when the teachers encourage grappling, the claims frequently outrun the reality. The opportunities for bluffing in both domains are substantial.

The difference lies in the ultimate objective. Advertisers want the observer to buy the product. It is a simpler objective, and if achieved, it is easily measured. When the advertiser makes money, he considers himself a success. Educators have a more complex mission, a less measurable success rate. Although they sometimes try to engender enthusiasm and inspiration in their students, at other times they try to inculcate skepticism. They want the student to be able to stand up to the salesman—fully equipped to make a sound decision about whether and what to buy, be it a product, a political candidate, or an idea.

To do this, the student must grapple, must understand efficiency and corner-cutting and bluffing—the uses and the dangers of each. There are circumstances where even the tiniest deception has no place. We do not want our surgeon to bluff. Or our carpenter. Or our bank. Or our police officer. From them, we want and expect the unvarnished truth, without any sort of cosmetic treatment. The world depends on honest answers coming from clear minds.

Schools are both intensely personal and intensely social places. They are personal in their attempts to help children to develop their minds. Minds are very private places: they need to be kept clear, sharp, straightforward. Since the essential pur-

pose of school is to create a rational and thoughtful citizenry, it
needs to be a place of honesty and precision.

But schools are also social places, places where children
come out of their homes to learn to relate with other children
and with adults who are not their parents. In social life, some
dishonesty is acceptable—even welcome. One may cheerfully
play with a kid one doesn't really like, or keep quiet when one
would really rather talk, or accept without any real evidence a
teacher's judgment that progress in one's reading or writing is
just around the corner. These are the half-truths that make
people free—well, maybe not free, but stronger. And another
basic purpose of school is to make kids stronger and more confident.

Teachers can and must handle these dual purposes of
schooling, not by throwing their hands up in despair or finding
a way to blame college teachers or politicians or even the children's parents, but by reveling in the complexity and the purpose which makes their craft so much more important than
those of so many other people. Admirable schools look at themselves carefully to be sure that they are set up to encourage honesty. They "cheat-proof" both homework and tests by making
each one as individual as possible, by tying each to a respectable
task which the student understands and respects. They tolerate
bluffing only when there is a clear and acknowledged social purpose. They struggle to avoid those other, corrosive sorts of
bluffing which signal toleration, and thereby approbation, of
practices which deliberately mislead.

WHY DOES Angela kvetch about her assignment? One reason is that she is fifteen and would rather watch a show
on TV than try to figure out what Hemingway meant by his old

man, the sea, and a fish. Careful interpretive reading is hard work, requiring intellectual sweat. None of us of any age wants to do such work all the time, especially after a busy, exhausting day.

Angela's "homework" is to be done at night, after such a hard day. Further, no two bits of it are connected. The math has nothing to do with the biology, and the French has nothing to do with the English. It is to be done alone, apart from the stimulation of others.

In many cases, homework is done with guidelines provided by teachers, but in this case, none had been provided. Compounding this confusion is the reality that the expectations of the teachers usually vary widely. The overall result is a menu of evening obligations in the form of a disparate list of Things To Do. There is no overall reason for it all, save the necessity of accomplishing enough to avoid embarrassment the following day.

Quiet, sustained attention is tough for any of us, but especially so for a teenager who has little experience of the benefits of sticking hard to important things and who sees adults at home sinking into the couch and having a beer in front of the television at the same time that she is expected to be plumbing meaning from what is to her an utterly murky text.

So Angela procrastinates. So would most adults. And she and most adults would quickly figure out how to bluff through the next day.

And Elaine cuts corners with her 10c class. Her life is divided into sharply different spheres. When she is with 10c, Janey and Neal and Bob and Duchess must be out of her mind. But when she is with the children, 10c presumes to intrude. Serious teaching does not carry an eight-to-four expectation, whatever any contract says. The thinking and planning about how to teach Hemingway to a particular group of tenth graders must be done in all too many American schools largely beyond the formal schoolday. It is a day which for Elaine is jammed with a procession of classes; she has over nine dozen students and neither the time nor the place for thinking about teaching. And if that thinking about teaching is not accomplished at school, it must be done at home. If it can't be done at home, bluffing becomes necessary.

Elaine resents this reality, but it persists. So she, too, procrastinates, figuring out how to fake it, how to bluff her way through.

Angela and Elaine are not exceptions within American high schools. Indeed, they are the rule. Veteran educators know this. They worry about it. But the ways and the will to address it seem endlessly out of reach.

No one wants schoolpeople or schoolchildren to get into the habit of cutting corners. A dependence on such artfulness undercuts the basic premise of the life of the mind. No school would take pride in such a lesson. A school which appears in its activity, however unintentionally, actually to tolerate—even value—bluffing teaches a dangerous and academically corrupt lesson.

Concerned schools can look carefully for those places where the temptation to bluff (in the worst sense) is powerful. A school's quest for greater consistency in its message can start with seven questions:

Is more expected of both students and teachers than it is possible for most to do well?

The primary cause of bluffing is overload, as in Elaine's case. Since there is too much to do, much is done superficially. Quantity is the enemy of quality.

Of course, what is too much for me is not too much for you. Ironically, homework is often designed to give the slower students a little more time than others might need. Johnny, who reads quickly, may take more time with math. He can adjust his preparations to his own needs. In that way, the class discussion can start on what is more nearly a level playing field.

Further, and equally obviously, no school wants to be a place for goof-offs. Schools have to have high standards and that means that they have to discriminate. Each child may work differently, but each child should work hard. Everyone should be pushed to do deeply effective work—not just lots of work—but effective work takes time.

Such a complicated agenda is not met by typical American high school policy. Indeed, much policy runs counter to the notion of individualized, high standards. Instead, policy makes a virtue out of standardization. Most schools depend on a predictable regimen, for students and adults alike. Most schools offer a cornucopia of opportunities—a seven-period day, with something different in at least six of those periods, a blizzard of extracurricular activities, off-campus programs such as Community Service, vacation trips for French classes to Quebec—all in a swirl of busy-ness.

Everyone is expected to flourish under this regimen. There are kudos for those who appear to do the most. And grades are given, but there is little careful thought about the real and lasting quality of what has been accomplished, a fact that is readily understood by the students. Once a class or activity is over, it is over. There is no requirement that a worthy residue remain to be drawn upon at some later date.

Too much usually means too little. The little comes from bluffing, from pretending to be on top of things rather than being their master. Schools which can teach their students the difference between superficiality and substance, by contrast, are focused but flexible places, and they have taught important, lifelong lessons.

Do conditions in the school allow each student to be known well?

That is, is each student known well enough by his teachers so that if he is bluffing, they can quickly deal with it? Does each teacher have a student and class load which makes knowing each student well a reasonable possibility?

Anonymity is the curse of good teaching and inevitably contributes to corner-cutting. If no one knows the students in a high school, it is easy for them to drift through. They may even believe that they prefer the anonymity. At least in the short run, it certainly makes it easier to fool folks. And it yields the time to deal with other parts of their lives: the social, the emotional, the financial, all of which seem very important, none of which has much to do with the lessons to be taught by an old fisherman.

There is no point trying to deal with the curse of the corrosive kind of bluffing if the school's adults can't get beyond the mere names of their students. What is a proper load of students for a single teacher? Elaine's 118 is clearly too many. Most critics say that the number for a veteran must be below 100. Wealthy parents will pay thousands of dollars a year to have their offspring taught by teachers who carry loads of 70 or fewer.

Teacher load—total load of students-to-get-to-know, not just "class size"—is in so many school systems so out of line that it rarely is faced squarely. In many schools, where 150 to 200 is the norm, 118 would be a joy. To get the numbers down for Elaine will require either adding money to the budget or substantially reallocating what is now available. Both would provoke strong political reactions. The failure to face up to this critical situation, or even to mention it, sends a powerful signal to students that adults have no stomach to address painful issues that profoundly affect those students' lives. In this, there is a moral message.

How does this school pace itself? Is there time to work, time to reflect, and time to rest?

The hours when students and teachers are freshest are the hours when the most demanding intellectual and imaginative work most effectively takes place. This usually means the earlier hours, or the hours after a refreshing break. The most difficult work tends to be the most intense; and the most intense work tends to be the most personally engaging and, inevitably, threatening.

Recent research has indicated that for reasons of physiological development, what is "productively early" for a teenager may be a few hours later than for an adult. The 7:00 A.M. adolescent sleepiness with which all teachers are familiar may reflect more than just youngsters' night-owl predilections. 9:00 A.M. may be a better starting time than the familiar 7:30 or 8:00. Such a time schedule may serve adults better as well, albeit for reasons of family convenience rather than physiological development. Whether 7:30 or 9:00, the best hours for most people doing their most serious work will be the first ones in the formal schoolday.

The initial careful reading of a difficult text is not best done as end-of-the-day homework, as Angela demonstrated. Reviewing the text and considering some questions about it might be better then. Even better might be discussing the text; a sociable but nonetheless purposeful conversation can be constructive even at the end of a long day.

Most schools put the conversation first and the quiet, individual work at the end. Administratively inconvenient or not, this is backward. A look at most productive adult intellectual activity makes that point.

Pace relates to calendar. Late September, October, and April are, in many corners of this country, usually more productive teaching times than are pre-holiday, flu-ridden winter and early summer weeks. An efficient school would capitalize on the better times and make the best possible use of the less productive. Again, this is bureaucratically a nuisance. A standard "term" is easier to schedule and easier for those engaged in traditional collective bargaining. Failure to take account of the flow of a year increases the chances of missing opportunities in good times and cutting corners, including bluffing, in bad.

Are the expectations for students and teachers clear?

If you do not know clearly what is expected, it is hard to prepare, hard to focus. It is easy to give everything a once-over-lightly, leaving any demonstration of mastery thereafter to adroit bluffing. While too much "clarity" snuffs out imagination, too little makes a task seem either hopelessly broad or meaningless in its lack of definition. Angela had merely to "read" thirty pages. A provocative question which could only be answered by delving into those pages might have provoked useful effort.

An assignment which is put merely in terms of coverage unadorned with a persuasive reason for the assignment—"Do every third problem on page 165," or "Read Chapter Two"— fails to provoke interest, and boredom is the enemy of serious work. Lively questions make for lively answers. Most students have the impression that they are given homework just to keep them at their desks for the evening, out of their parents' hair. They can't see where their work tonight will contribute to a more interesting class tomorrow. All this is fuel for the habit of bluffing.

Is there time during the school day for reflection and for quiet work?

Angela needed time to read. So did Elaine. Reading and time for careful analysis is important time. Few schools allow much for it during the day. Reading is for later, they imply. And later is being more tired, further from relevant conversation and in home settings which may be noisy and confusing. One wonders how a law firm would prosper if between nine and five everyone in the firm was at nonstop but disparate meetings, with no time to make sense of the problems before them.

Much of a young person's work that counts academically takes place in private time—the minutes or hours during which puzzlement can become understanding. However, many believe that the typically frenetic schoolday is a necessity born of adolescence: if they aren't given Things To Do at a fast pace, the adolescent inmates will act up.

This is a self-fulfilling prophecy. One need look no further than the shops of a strong vocational/technical program or the silent intensity of a computer laboratory to see the ability and willingness—even the demand—of young people to be allowed to get on with their work. Such intensity is born of a focus on some compelling problem and an expectation on the part of adults that young people can do serious, sustained work. This sort of expectation is difficult to "command" from the principal's office of a massive high school. It grows only in settings where the adults and the students know each other well.

Serious, sustained intellectual activity is a new experience for most teenagers. It does not come easy; they do not know how best to use it and, early on, become frustrated. But of such effort arises the competence that academic work at a worthy secondary school can encourage. A school which makes it possible is one likely to have strong students—and ones who are less likely to need to bluff.

A school which values and protects quiet time as part of its day-long regimen addresses Elaine's problems as much as Angela's. Elaine would have known that she had some minutes to gather her wits around *The Old Man and the Sea* before 10c's meeting, minutes free of her family's demands and the essays for 11B. She would be far less likely to need to bluff.

When compared with serious adult workplaces, the high school is exceptional in its unceasing busy-ness. It is a place full of everybody going from here to there every hour. A cold-eyed observer would—at the least—call it a massively inefficient use of time. The damage done to thorough work, and the habit of doing thorough work, would take longer to see, but it is there. And thorough work makes the habit of bluffing unnecessary.

Are the incentives and opportunities for clearly demonstrated work clear and pervasive within a school?

If sloppy work is acceptable, bluffing is a sensible strategy for both students and teachers. Of course, a "sloppy" assignment for one teacher is a "necessarily flexible" assignment for another; and too much precision in the definition of a sensible answer can smother imagination and initiative. If the assignments are too long and the curricular ground to be covered too broad, the necessity for superficial work, by teachers and students alike, is high. That is fertile ground for dishonesty.

If the school's most critical tests are relatively unconnected to the immediate, daily work in school, and if these assessments do not require many demanding skills (such as clear, graceful writing), then the incentive to ease off on those activities will be irresistible. If the tests-that-count, for example, are all of the multiple-choice variety, then the effort of students and teachers to master more complex and varied tasks will be sapped. Only the barest minimum of that kind of work will done—because it "doesn't count." Faking it will become epidemic.

In its presentation and recommendation of students for
college admission and job placement, does the school
absolutely insist on accuracy as well as advocacy?

Every school wants to be and should be its students' advocates, but not at the expense of integrity. Most teachers care for their students and believe that they will succeed in the future even more consistently than they are succeeding in high school. Positive recommendations along those lines are not dishonest.

There is considerable pressure on high schools, however, to let students pile up largely fictitious "extracurricular offices" or to rewrite the student's "personal statement" for college admissions. Seeming to conspire in a student's presentation of herself as someone who she is not signals to the student and to others that creative lying—bluffing, as it were—is acceptable. And to justify such activities by saying that "the colleges expect this puffery" compounds the felony.

The adolescents watch us all the time. If the institution and its adult leaders play the bluffing game, whether baldly as with college admissions or almost unconsciously by insisting on completely unrealistic "coverage" in the curriculum, the students will quickly learn that a superficial dip into ideas, matched with a cool ability to fake understanding, is what serious intellectual life is all about.

Bluffing, then, is not just a problem of "lying." It goes much deeper. Students who are trying to be honest people should avoid it, at least where it is as self-serving as it was in Angela's case. However, it is first and foremost an adult problem, a systemic problem, not one merely of adolescent morals. Schools where everyone is in the habit merely of "getting by," for whatever worthy reasons, are conspirators for any sort of unworthy work and the dishonesty that it provokes. Such schools need to take a close and brutal look at themselves.

The problem does not lie only with Angela and Elaine as individuals. If the schools' leaders believe so, they are bluffing themselves.

4 *Sorting*

SOMETIMES Tom feels that there isn't anything he can do about it. He is in eighth grade and suddenly there are all these challenges to face, like deciding what high school to attend. Should he take the test for the magnet school of Arts and Sciences? Or not take the test and just go to West High, his neighborhood comprehensive high school? Or should he give in to his grandmother and apply for admission to Seven Acres Academy, a private school? Granny said she'd pay.

He has done pretty well in some subjects, science and mathematics especially, and he appreciates it when those classes have good teachers. Math is great. In that class he only has to know the facts. Is the answer plus ten or minus ten? He bet he could do well in English and social studies, but the classes are boring and the teachers keep asking him his opinion about why things happened. How can he answer a question like that? Would his opinions matter even if he had them? He doesn't know—or care—anything about all that faraway stuff. No one else in class does either, so they just gas on about nothing.

Since he likes to make things, maybe he should go to technical school. People said that the Voc was for poor kids, and he's not poor. Not rich, really. But his friends would not be going to the Voc. Maybe he could talk some of them into it. They could all go together. Maybe he could sign up for West High and still take some courses at the Voc. Somebody said that anyone could do that. West has tracks, which means that a group of kids stay together for most of their courses. He could pick a track that connected with the Voc. However, maybe the teachers pick the track for you. Just like the Magnet, where you have to pass exams. He would be sorted out by means of the scores, Voc or no Voc on the basis of some numbers that summed him up. Boring, stupid, unfair! He will need to choose, but he doesn't want to be sorted. Sorting is done *to* you.

Does he want to go to college? If so, what sort of college? His parents will hassle him about all this because they want him to go to college no matter what. He has to face it: they expect to be partners in his decision whether he likes it or not. They might even dangle inducements, like Granny did about Seven Acres Academy.

All that college stuff seems so far away and yet it's on a lot of people's minds. He wishes it weren't. He wishes he could stay just where he is, lumped in with everyone else. He doesn't want to be surrounded by mostly-rich or mostly-poor kids. He doesn't want to get started in a certain kind of school, even the big-deal magnet school, and find out that it is not right for him. He is afraid of being considered a certain kind of kid, maybe even a kid he really doesn't want to be. He doesn't want to displease his parents, but he doesn't want them to make the decisions for him. Wherever he goes, he doesn't want to be cut off from his friends. Isn't this the only important thing? He can't learn without his friends, but, no matter what he chooses, some of his friends will choose something else.

Why does he have to choose? Why can't things go on just as they are now? Why is everybody suddenly so concerned? Why are all these different people putting him in boxes? Why does so much about high school have to be about sorting?

THE VISITOR had lunch with a group of fourteen- and fifteen-year-olds, black, white, and Hispanic, male and female, at a small public "alternative" school in a big city. Lincoln was a relatively small and new school, as city high schools go.

"Why did you choose to come to this school?" the visitor asked.

"I flunked the exam for the academic magnet school. My mother made me."

"Why?" the visitor followed up. "What was your mother's reasoning?"

"She just made me." The youngster wouldn't budge beyond that.

Another voice: "My mother made me too, but I like being here because of the cafeteria." The eatery was full of older people, people who seemed very busy and serious. "But I didn't come for that." This was a young Hispanic girl, struggling with her English. "I came because I hated Catholic school and my parents wouldn't let me stay in the public school because I was messing up." This school *is* a public school, but since it's not large and it's not in the neighborhood, she didn't think of it that way.

Another answer: "I needed to change my life, get away from the gangs. In fact, I ran a gang in middle school. This school is helping me stay out of trouble." The visitor followed up with this white girl. "How is this school helping?" "They let me start here without a rep, I mean a reputation. They know me here. They know how to help me. But I know I'll need more help before I'm through here."

A serious black male spoke next. "It's a lot more work in this school. That's why some kids leave after the first year. But I want to go to college."

Now a young white male, a kid now living largely on his own. "I've been to a lot of schools. Two schools ago, they went out of business and lost all my records. I had to find another school anyway. I thought this one was friendlier than the other one I got into."

The students described their school with pride. "They make us work hard here, but they help us with it." "And they understand when we need a break. Last week, after the science fair, we got to watch a movie." "But even when we watch a movie, we have to write a journal about it."

The visitor was excited by the students' appreciation, by their sense of ownership, by how well they understood their teachers' motives. She turned to the only student who had not spoken yet. "Why did you come here?" The student looked the visitor over somewhat skeptically. Finally, she answered, "Me? It's near the subway."

SORTING STARTS early in life: prenatally, even, when one's mother eats well or abuses alcohol during the pregnancy. Once a child is born, the story is about careful or careless child tending, good or bad nutrition, welcoming or frightening schools. When the time comes to choose one's high school, each student has more or fewer options depending on his record, his wealth, the part of the country he lives in. Even where there are several options, she has probably already developed a pattern of decision-making in which more or fewer factors are taken into account. The way the choice of high schools is made usually has a large influence on its outcome. Some students make the decision themselves after considerable research and self-knowledge; others move along with the crowd; still others do what their parents think they should do. Some kids are happy enough to admit that their parents were right; others put a lot of energy into proving them wrong.

Even after a high school is chosen, more sorting needs to go on before a student feels comfortable in it. Another cafeteria we visit serves a small city's only high school. In some ways, it would be the answer to Tom's prayers: no choice needed. It is a friendly place which enrolls some 1800 students. The clatter and chatter are overwhelming, but charming in their way. There is a noisy air of good feelings. A few teachers on "cafeteria duty" hang around, chatting with each other or with clots of students at a particular table. The rest of the teachers share a glassed-in alcove, the faculty dining room.

The food lines are off to the side. There is variety from which to choose, a series of outposts of well-known fast food marts. Burger King. A fried chicken outlet and one for pizza. There is a salad bar, a magnet for girls and faculty members. Marriott provides the traditional fare. Kids on "free or reduced lunch," compliments of the federal government, must use that line. Sorting occurs even here.

Closer observation of all this happy hubbub tells us more. There is a sociology to the long eating tables, each served by individual metal stools levered from under the tabletop. There are several distinct groups, each one totally engrossed in its own world. After a morning ranging over a large high school, these lunch friends make the cafeteria feel like home. Over there to our left is an overcrowded table made up entirely of younger white girls, all talking at once. Ninth graders from South Middle School, we are told. Over here is a table of three distinct groups: some younger black boys, a mix of kids whom a teacher identified as track enthusiasts, and some older, noisy black kids, male and female.

In the middle is a quiet table of youngsters eating alone or in pairs. On the corner are what a teacher called the beautiful people, regal and assured older kids, conservatively dressed, largely but not exclusively white. It is with them, and with a knot of kids who are termed "science nerds," that the supervising teachers periodically sit.

As we leave the cafeteria, we notice a few youngsters, mostly younger boys, eating quietly alone in the alcoves carved out of the school's long hallways. They have brought their lunches from home, and seem to be savoring the familiar food and the peace so much that they don't mind the loneliness. In a classroom we pass we see the chess club, sitting on the floor, munching sandwiches while intently staring at the boards in play. Their sandwiches could be cardboard for the attention the eaters pay them.

"We have nice kids here," we are told by teachers. Certainly the kids appear so, and that is a relief. The social sorting in high school can be especially brutal. Even here, clearly all was not as friendly, pleasant, and self-chosen as it appeared. The very regularity of the lunch groups indicates caution and fear as much as stability. There must be plenty of kids who want to switch groups, if only for a day, who don't dare. However, these groups—and even the nongroups—seemed to be offering the students a haven they needed, a sense of their own context, of their own identity. And no one would begrudge them that.

We settle in the faculty dining room, which is filled with round tables, each seating some half-dozen people. At one table some older women are talking quietly among themselves. Next to them is a noisy group, mostly men; their talk is of some recent disturbance at school. At yet another is a clutch of younger teachers, men and women. We join the principal and the assistant principals. Our talk turns to the twin evils of rigid academic tracking and the predicament faced by teachers struggling to do well by "heterogeneously" grouped classrooms. The better teachers know their students, the more daunted they feel by their remarkably different skills, intellectual maturity, and interest in going to school. It is hard to plan an hour which would be useful to all of them.

The principal outlines his dilemma. This school believes that every kid is unique, that every kid should be all that she or he can be, and that students must not be sorted out too quickly by test scores or other methods. In a democracy one works with people from every quarter. Well, maybe not "works with," but depends on. Segregation is the great American curse. In this city, he argues, we are lucky to have only one high school. Everyone attends. The school gives this city its glue. Everyone has a chance here. We believe in excellence.

However, the fact remains that some of the ninth graders can't read or even do division. Some of the older girls are already mothers. They face special challenges in trying to concentrate. And, he has to admit, the kids from the different feeder schools tend to be in the same classes.

"Do you track the kids academically?" we ask.

"We have to. The parents want it."

"All parents?"

"No. The parents of the academically talented are politically powerful. We must have our separated honors track because they insist on it."

"Are the kids in the honors track a cross-section of the student body?"

"No. They are mostly white kids from the eastern side of town."

"Who lives on the eastern side of town?"

"The richer families."

"Is this democratic, in the melting-pot sense you say you admire?"

"Our school isn't perfect. But, yes, we can live with it. The kids are all under the same roof. They mix in the hallways, in the cafeteria."

"Do they? Look out the window onto those long tables. Haven't they sorted themselves out, 'tracked' themselves?"

"We don't like the black kids always eating by themselves."

"Is it equally bad for the ninth-grade white girls always to eat by themselves?"

"That's different."

"How different?"

"The faculty don't like the segregation. We work against it."

"Is the faculty dining room in fact itself segregated?"

"That's different."

"How different?"

IT IS human nature to sort ourselves out. We gather with people who are congenial. Or we gather with blood relatives, whether or not they are congenial. Or we gather with people who speak our language, share our passions, vibe with us in some way, laugh at our jokes, deserve our trust. These kinds of sorting are expected in a free society.

Within a school, sorting may well be informal, the result of the shifting and sliding of friends and associates of all ages. Schools, like neighborhoods, are replete with what could be called *benign* ways of sorting, the gathering of people in circles which invigorate them at little or no cost to any or many others. The chess players, the younger teachers munching their lunch together, the giggling white ninth-grade girls, the track enthusiasts, or the black kids who are kidding each other are examples.

When students choose a particular school—the Lincoln High School, for example—they engage in another kind of largely benign sorting. For a host of reasons they, or their parents, choose this place rather than another. The reasons may be social on the kids' parts, academic on their parents', or vice versa. They may shift over time. This choice does not simply drop into their laps, obviously. Kids and parents have aggressively to find out about the school, get in line as applicants, and clear the way to admission. A child without an adult behind him or her is at a disadvantage, and in this respect the process is not benign: the young person without an advocate is likely to get lost.

The puzzled eighth grader, trying to decide where to go next year, also exemplifies the process of benign sorting. A city may offer a variety of high schools, and, as Tom is finding out to his dismay, each one carries with it an aura of decision-making about his future work and life. The decision he and his parents ultimately make (with Granny's help, perhaps) will be important to him, but his choice of it will affect others only marginally, if at all. If he chooses a private school, his parents may become less interested in the public schools, but they will continue to pay their town's taxes.

When an eighth grader can choose among a variety of high schools, such sorting as occurs need not be seen as a zero-sum game: limited access to a scarce resource. It can be seen against the overall goal of an excellent education for all.

PITY THE high school: it is expected to bring order, yet is crammed full of disorderly people. Its announced goals are to help students concentrate in their classrooms, but it still needs to get those cheerleaders out in the parking lot by two o'clock sharp so that they will be on time for their away game. In this and other instances, learning conflicts with order and loses; the public address system advertises the school's real—if reluctant and unacknowledged—priorities.

It is the search for order which produces so many sorting devices. Some are built around chronological age and disciplinary boundaries. You are thirteen and so it is time for you to make a high school decision. You are fifteen and so you are most likely a "tenth grader." Or you are a teacher who majored in English in college and so you teach English here in the high school. These bases for sorting are both obvious on their faces and of long tradition.

Of course, both can have deep and obvious flaws. No one of us grows intellectually at the same rate and in the same way. How old we are tells us something about where we are intellectually and socially but rarely all that is important about each of us. "English" as a subject has myriad definitions. I may not know what I need to know in order to teach well, and the disciplinary separations between "English" and other languages and literatures, history and the arts are deep. Thus, even with my degree in English, I may be utterly unprepared to teach what the children actually need. The mere completion of a college "major" tells us something but hardly everything that is important.

At other times, the reasons for sorting arise from governmental requirements that schools achieve racial balance. Most of this managerial sorting usually flows from policy decisions and generally follows specific rules to make the assignments as scrupulously "fair" as possible. Balance and fairness may well be moral ends; they may reflect the will of the people as a whole and thus be democratic. If the policy is imposed from "above," however—from a superintendent's office, a legislature, or a judge—it will be perceived as coming from administrators rather than from the people affected. The reasons behind such sorting may not be appreciated, especially by a teenager who has been cut off from his friends.

T HE COLLEGE president at the convocation for incoming first-year students told them how wonderful they were. A quarter of them ranked first, second, or third in their high school graduating classes. Most were in the top quarter of their secondary school's scholars. Collectively they displayed the highest average SAT scores in the college's history. They were, he told them, an elite, a national resource.

High school had exquisitely sorted them out from their purportedly less able peers. This sorting has a long history in America. In his *Notes on the State of Virginia,* recommending a system of schools to be operated at public expense, Thomas Jefferson put it bluntly: by a system of "trials . . . the best geniuses will be raked from the rubbish annually." Only the deserving could proceed with a formal education.

Who is part of the elite and who is "rubbish"? Does a student with A's in senior English, history, art, geology, and third-year French rank higher than a student who has A's in senior English, fourth-year German, and music composition and A-minuses in AP (Advanced Placement) calculus and a biology research seminar? How ranks the nineteen-year-old recent immigrant from Cambodia who has a B-minus in "accelerated sophomore" English composition, an A-minus in fourth-year French, and A's in AP Calculus (the so-called BC examination), AP physics, and AP biology?

Most competitive high schools "weight" courses. An A in a fourth-year Spanish course might count for "1," with "Spanish Seminar" counting for "1.2," and Modern Dance counting for "0.7." The valedictorian and the salutatorian—the first and second ranking students—may be separated by a hundredth of a decimal point. One is Number One. The other is not. That sorting is supposed to mean something about intellectual excellence.

How does the all-A student from West High School rank against an all A-minus student at the academic magnet school? Or an all-A student at the small, private Seven Acres Academy?

Is an A the same from each of these schools? Or even from two teachers within one of these schools? Students in one school may feel superior to those in another because their grades are better. In that case, they assume that they have become interested in learning so their work is improving. Others, however, may feel superior because their grades are worse. It was so easy to earn A's in their old school, but in this one they really have to get down to work. There are many different ways of comparing schools, but grades don't seem to be a reliable way to do it.

Still, the urge to sort compels one to persist. Some compare students across schools on the basis of scores on common standardized tests such as those administered by the College Board or the American College Testing Service. These tests are administered at the same time and demand the attention of each student for no more than three or four hours at most. Some young people do well in such hothouse assessment situations. Some do not. Such tests discriminate in favor of those for whom this assessment routine is congenial and who may have been drilled to do well in this examination format. Most of these external tests, forced to use a format that can be "graded" by machines, necessarily present but a slice of the discipline, those aspects of the subject which lend themselves to such a testing regimen.

Whatever the routine, academic sorting happens, and much of it follows social sorting. The relatively benign atmosphere of the cafeteria gives way to a tougher purpose in the academic classes. There are winners and losers. In most high schools, adolescents are ranked, one better than the other, and these rankings affect their future prospects.

THESE ARE the images which have made Tom's parents and grandmother so nervous about the choice he will make, or at least will need to buy into. Admission to the magnet school is complicated. An eighth grader and his parents must, in the first instance, want him to go; they must be informed and organized and take the initiative to apply. Admission usually turns on some judgment about an applicant's academic promise, and that "promise" is usually gauged by performance on specific examinations or on "class rank" at a middle school. Sometimes teacher recommendations are also expected.

There is potential bias in all of these mechanisms. Save at the extremes—such as when the student is demonstrably semi-literate or is not only clearly literate but deep in his reading and graceful in his writing—one-shot examinations are a poor predictor of future academic success. Even the fabled Scholastic Achievement Test of the College Board correlates usefully with university performance only for the first two semesters of work. After that, there is little correlation between scores and academic prowess, let alone future career prospects.

Teachers' recommendations are equally flawed, though they too are useful at the margins. A student may be well or not well known, an "agin-the-government" type or a faculty groupie; or the teacher writing the report might do so casually or unintelligibly. And so the traditional devices for selection, however carefully the system may try to be even-handed, are less than benign. Most traditional indices, for a host of reasons, favor the children coming from secure homes and families of means.

These *are* good children—don't get us wrong; some of our best friends were and are these kinds of children—and they deserve all the institutional support we can offer them. They are also more likely to fit into a school's routines and to agree with its purposes. They are not, however, the only good children who are of concern to us, and their schools are not the only context in which a child might profitably learn. If we have "one best system," and if we insist that each child in the nation conform to its strictures, we will effectively give up our search for better ways to reach all kinds of learners. Unless the nation as a whole supports a variety of educational options, it will not support all its children as we in a democracy claim to be doing.

This is what makes the "tracking" experience in high school so crucial for so many youngsters; it becomes go along or get out, with both options impossible ones. Someone can always get hurt by being misplaced. The issue in a school is the degree of hurt that is suffered by how many students or faculty, and how long that hurt will last.

In an effort to reduce that hurt, many American high schools let the students sort themselves out academically. They term themselves "comprehensive" and offer a variety of opportunities from among which students may choose. Some of the elite options—an honors track, for instance—require a prior record of high achievement. Others expect only a statement of interest, however tepid. High school is thus filled with various kinds of programs, each carrying its own demand for hard (or not so hard) work, prestige and reputation. The process of parents advising and pushing, school authorities testing and counseling, and students choosing sorts a school out, in a deliberate and usually congenial way. There is not much of a common agenda expected of all the students. Most students have to do no more in school than most of them wish, or at least no more than the adults advising them believe they can do. Not surprisingly, the various programs in a high school are like the various stores in a shopping mall, some upscale, some not—the honors program, the various "shop" courses, a "business" track and more—and they end up reflecting social class and ethnic lines.

The process is deliberate and politically tolerable. The young people—and their parents—who want certain kinds of choices get them. Those who for whatever reason don't insist on certain choices still have an opportunity to "choose." When the state imposes standardized tests for all students at a certain grade level, the kids in the honors track do well, and the young people in the other tracks do less well, and no one is surprised. It even seems to confirm the legitimacy of "one best system."

The process of careful sorting required in a thoughtful school is inevitably excruciating. Schools require a logical structure. However, students, even those of the same age, are not all alike, in energy, intellectual acuity, interests, or social and emotional maturity. Further, the students change. Yesterday's distracted sluggard is today's newly charged up zealot, at least about something. And teachers themselves cannot be neatly pigeonholed. Accordingly, a school which asserts that everyone will proceed in that school in a carefully prescribed way at all times is profoundly discriminatory, and thereby extraordinarily ineffective. Such schools have a patina of toughness and focus. But they make the same mistake that a doctor makes who prescribes two aspirins and lots of water for every patient who complains of a headache.

Some sorting is profoundly destructive. The rigid academic "tracking" so common in American high schools has been demonstrated to be harmful in research study after research study, but it nonetheless persists. It is attractive to families who want their children segregated by race, class, or other stereotype within a larger school. It is desirable for the parent who wants his child to be with more serious students. And it is efficient for the teacher who wants to reduce the variety in her classroom so she can create more workable lesson plans.

However, the evidence is overwhelming that categorical tracking into faster classes doesn't necessarily improve learning, and tracking into slower classes becomes a self-fulfilling prophecy. Challenge a student only a little and you will get small results. Challenge the same student appropriately but formally, and you will get much better results. The Army recruiter's cliché, "Be All That You Can Be," has within it a profound and useful message for schoolpeople.

The paradox here is that to be fair and responsible a school has to be "tracked," in the sense that it places each student in the setting that serves him or her best at a particular time. A truly honest school is massively tracked, with every student at his or her most appropriate place at any moment—being asked insistently to be all that each one can be. To do so is, of course, an administrative nightmare, but one that has to be faced and which has been more forthrightly faced in other large-scale professions. Wartime armies have little strict age-grouping. It is performance that counts.

How would individual tracking work? How can each student be challenged to work as hard as he can? Gil, a seventeen-year-old student, is reviewing his portfolio of work with his adviser. The portfolio is a collection of what he and his teacher consider his best work over the last six months. Persuading a committee of his growing academic abilities is required for "promotion" to Thoreau School's "senior division." He also has to prepare an "argument" on an important topic, make that argument in a written and, as necessary, illustrated essay, and then "defend" it orally before a group of adults informed about the topic and some of his classmates.

Last spring, Gil's adviser had not recommended that he present his work for consideration. She had believed that it was not up to standard. Gil's parents complained, largely on the grounds that Gil was "old for his class," that he "tried hard," and that he thereby deserved to be "promoted." Holding him "back" was "demoralizing him." The parents felt that Gil would now simply throw in the towel. A group of faculty members had reviewed Gil's work, discussed it with Gil and his adviser, and held firm. Gil had not met the "intermediate" standard. Gil's parents angrily complained. If they had been wealthier, they probably would have engaged a lawyer to present their views. Gil returned in the fall still in the intermediate division.

Gil's adviser kept pressing him on his required "analytic essays," pieces of writing which took a text of some sort—an op-ed piece from a newspaper, the transcript of a C-Span debate over the morality of "athletic scholarships" at the state university, a review of Chinua Achebe's *Things Fall Apart*—and subjected it to a close reading and critique.

"You need better ones, Gil. These won't sell."

"But I can't. I don't have time. I hate doing these analytic pieces. Let me do some more poetry . . . Rap . . ."

"You won't pass with more of that. You do that well. They reflect you well, your ideas. But the panel will want to see how you take someone else's ideas apart and weigh them."

Gil responded angrily. *"Why?"*

"That's the real world, Gil. If you don't understand other people's ideas, *really* get them, they will sell you a bill of goods."

Gil scowled. He wasn't convinced.

"You want people to read and understand your poetry, don't you, Gil? You want people to pay attention to your ideas . . ."

More scowl.

Finally. "O.K., sure . . ."

"Other people want no less care paid to their arguments and poems than you do."

The adviser's appeal was rational but not persuasive to Gil, at least not to an extent that would send him back to the library for a book or journal and a word processor there. What sent Gil there—finally—was the fear of not passing, and thus not getting promoted. He went. He produced two additional essays, in quick order. Gil and his adviser went over each one, draft by draft. The portfolio, still shaky at the edges, had some fresh substance. There was genuine rigor to this process, as opposed to formulaic gate-keeping.

Gil's adviser threatened. The entire routine of the school threatened. To get ahead you had to present your work for public scrutiny, even from some adults who have never met you. The school's very system built in that pressure.

But the adviser also supported and played to his strength—his desire to write poetry which would be understood. Gil was also told where some of his weaknesses lay. He was helped to strengthen them. He was treated as a particular person, not as one of a class of "low scorers." He was not merely told that he had "failed." He was told why he needed to do more work, and he was helped onto a new level of work which was legitimately improved. He was never lied to about his talents or his failures. He accepted the onerous task of writing two more analytic papers because he trusted his school, even his seemingly ever-critical adviser, to make good on his improvement when it was finally displayed.

An athlete, Gil knew he was handled in his academic world much as he was handled in the basketball program. You won or you lost. Either way, you trained, worked hard, suffered a bit. Even basketball wasn't always fun. There was lots of sweat. But winning was an elixir. In basketball, the fear of losing powerfully focused the attention. In writing analytic essays, what made Gil put forth more effort was the prospect of being with the kids he wanted to be with. Underneath the social incentive, however, was at least some satisfaction with the job he did.

SORTING TAKES place everywhere in high schools, on many levels. Its purposes are usually well-meaning but rarely explained. The West High School social studies department met in early May to determine the criteria for its most admired students and then assign awards.

Who gets the prizes this year? There are several to be doled out. One is to be for the "best research essay by a senior." Another is for "a senior who most reflects the values exemplified by the life of Frances James," Ms. James having been a revered history teacher at the high school three decades earlier. Upon her death, some former students arranged for an annual prize to be given in her memory. A third is for "the best student of European History," an award dating back to the 1920s, when the flagship senior history course focused on "Europe Since 1815." Finally, there is the "Improvement" prize, "for a student from any class who has shown extraordinary growth in social studies."

The meeting starts with debate over the research essay. Several names are put forward for discussion. Two are predictable, those of a pair of hot-shot seniors who are the school's academic superstars across the curriculum. A third is that of a seventeen-year-old senior who had been at West only for nine months. He had previously attended a school in England where his family had been living while his father served at the U.S. Air Force base at Litchfield. This was a shy boy, devoted to his work in any subject where writing was assigned and valued. His English school had soaked him in writing assignments, and his work reflected that emphasis. A fourth student proposed for the prize was a tenth grader, one who, in the opinion of her teacher, had done extraordinary work, well beyond what was usually expected of a fifteen-year-old. "For a kid her age, she is a far more advanced scholar than are any of the seniors, given their ages . . ." argued

her advocates. "Isn't that what is meant by the 'best'?" they reasoned. The last student named was in the "college prep" track,
the academic level "below" the honors track, who had, with
substantial help and encouragement from her teacher, produced an essay way beyond her usual work. "If 'best' means
best effort, best work by this kid, then she deserves it," ex-
claimed this teacher.

How to sort these candidates out? Independent of the students, and applying the usual historical criteria, one of the essays by the two superstars would most likely win. But which
one? The essay by the newcomer from an English school was,
by American standards, quirky; it reflected the values dear to
his Litchfield teachers, values that had substantial integrity by
their own lights. If maturity and chronological age were to be
taken into account, the tenth grader easily won. If "being all
that you (now) can be" was taken into account, the college prep
student could win.

The department wrangled.

"Who gets a prize, and for what kind of work, sends a message to the rest of the school."

"The work alone should count. The situation or the age of
the writer is irrelevant."

"Kids who have been here for four years and who have
worked hard deserve the prizes."

"Let's look at all the prizes at once and spread them out
among the kids now on the table."

"Let's take into account the prizes that some kids will get
from other departments. A few kids shouldn't get all the school's
prizes. That wouldn't be fair."

"But if his history research essay was the best in the school,
what does it matter that he wins all sorts of other prizes?"

There were choices being made here about sorting, about

what the school values, about the quality of work and the quality of the effort to produce good work, about special situations in which some students find themselves and what meaning these have, about the fairness exhibited in the public awarding of honors, about understanding young people and what might energize them. The decisions being made would indicate respect for a certain kind of work or they would merely swell what might be some already excessively swollen heads.

The assumption is that prizes are important for the "signals they send" to the nonprizewinners. To those who, for now, have not achieved special recognition. To the many who have been sorted out rather than the few who have been sorted in. If the most important audience for the prize assembly are the students who need to be motivated to do more prizeworthy work, the best student to get the prize would be the one who started with the most disadvantages and managed to overcome them.

However, there are practical as well as pedagogical considerations in this form of sorting. The needs of the winners as well as of the losers need to be taken into consideration. What the department ultimately decides is to review students for all the awards at once, distributing them to spread the praise across those students the department most wants to honor. The principal demurs on two of them. He feels one student is getting too many prizes at graduation and that, for his benefit as well as for others, the department should choose another winner. He feels that awards should not be given to tenth graders, since it would lessen a senior's chance to be recognized. In any event, the tenth grader would not be at the graduation ceremony.

The department, already divided in making its initial recommendations, is annoyed by this intervention. However, the members are more comfortable complaining about the principal than arguing with each other. As in so many other matters, the argument strays off moral principle and into politics. High schools, besides being disorderly places, are also supremely human.

I N TRYING to decide upon a high school, Tom has stumbled into one of the most challenging aspects of growing up. The kids are old enough now to be acknowledged as different from each other, yet each one must be allowed to change and to keep his options open. The process of determining his goals and recognizing his own role in achieving them is painful for Tom, but it will strengthen him. His school can facilitate that process; it cannot control it and must not hinder it.

Sorting is a fact of life, and not necessarily a bad one. A sorting system which is flexible and reasonably respectful of people's wishes is essential. The trick is always to make the deliberate sorting as thoughtful as possible, harming as few people as possible. This takes care, time, flexibility, and patience and, because of that, it is expensive. All who pay those bills need to see the reason for them.

The high school that sorts appropriately will build so many advisers into its faculty that, sympathetically and in private, each student will have the chance to discuss her options as often as she wants. And while the faculty needs to be careful not to gossip about individuals, it should nevertheless be very public about its reasons for sorting in general, holding those reasons up to intense and unremitting scrutiny. How a school sorts teaches its students about discrimination and discriminating choices, about the gains and costs of attitudes ascribed and roads taken or not taken. When the society at large, or the administrative mechanisms of the educational system, insist on demonstrably harmful or indefensible sorting ("Who in this high school is Number One?"), the school community must be aware of these practices—and encouraged to protect their own policies. A school must not be forced to pit its students against each other. And, to the fullest extent possible, the school should openly, respectfully, and persistently refuse to be a party to the kind of discrimination which can bring permanent and unnecessary harm to any member of its community.

5 *Shoving*

SAMANTHA has to admit that she is always getting into trouble these days. She has grown so much in the last eighteen months that she bumps into people and things, often without meaning to. Actually, she secretly likes being bigger now, or at least not being tiny. She used to feel so weak, so powerless. Nobody even noticed her and she often felt squashed. Now she can look directly at her English teacher, and that's the way she likes it. Her teacher doesn't let on that this unnerves her, but Samantha believes that it must.

Samantha thinks that all the teachers are watching her more lately. They accuse her of shoving. That's the word they use for all kinds of things the kids do in school: teasing, back-slapping, rib-poking, piling into the auditorium together, even the high fives. "Samantha, stop shoving. Guys, ease up. Cool it, folks. Samantha! Stop shoving!" Samantha resents it.

The teachers in this school, she believes, have definitely lost their sense of humor. Maybe they never even had any. We don't do real shoving. That's when you are about to fight or when you deliberately hurt somebody. But we're just having a little fun, Samantha argues. Other people ought to understand that.

To shove is to push, to jostle. Shoving is a form of trespassing, going where you are not invited, crossing what are supposed to be boundaries, upsetting other people or things, showing that you are Big. Shoving off is different. It is leaving the scene instead of dominating it, but people often think of it as uncivil because they are startled. Shoving is generally perceived to be a bad thing.

However, the line between kidding around and malicious shoving is a fine one. A teammate's slap on the bottom of the football guard as he runs off the field is different than a male senior's slap on the bottom of a female sophomore in a crowded hallway. A poke in the ribs can be a form of saying "hi" or it can be a hurtful act. The difference is in the intentions of the poker and the expectations of the pokee.

Teachers cope with this ambiguity all the time.

"Who started this?"

"He poked me."

"Come on, I didn't poke you—not really. Not much."

Is it assault or simple horseplay? When did it turn physical? When did it turn intimidating? Who were the bystanders and how reliable is their witness? When she was young, Samantha tumbled around with boys. One day that stopped. Samantha is growing up. When the boys witlessly continue to roughhouse, she, her mother, and the teachers are outraged. A certain line, invisible but important, has been crossed.

Social class and ethnic and religious traditions help to determine where those lines are. Verbal horseplay in some groups is considered not only acceptable but desirable as a display of cleverness. Expressed exuberance—being "in your face"—is routine in some quarters, and not at all disrespectful. Silence is an expectation in other quarters. How close people stand to each other, whether they greet each other with a handshake or a kiss is a cultural act. Touching is *de rigeur* here and offensive there. This often bewildering variety of personal expression is part of the blessing and the curse of American diversity.

Shoving of all sorts is unrelenting in middle, junior high, and high schools. Most secondary school buildings are densely populated, the most peopled workplace that the majority of the students will ever experience in their lives. Physical shoving in the hallways is magnified because the Samanthas are getting bigger and, as they grow, clumsy, but some of her classmates are still quite small and thus intimidated. The situation is exacerbated during the so-called "passing times" because of the enforced quiet and attentive sitting which is expected in the classrooms. Adolescent muscles scream for liberation. The result is usually a physical and audible rush between classes which the adults may find unnecessarily raucous and even threatening.

Shoving is the invasion of another's space. At that level, stealing is a form of shoving. You take my book, since you have lost yours. I confront you. You say, "I just borrowed it. Hey, you know that." Steal or borrow, you pushed on to my turf, and without my permission. I try to be cool about it, but I carry around the feeling that you wronged me.

S AMANTHA'S SCHOOL tried to clear up disputes among the teenagers about physical shoving by asking a student group to consider and then publish what became a paper on "horseplay policy." The students did a sensible job of thinking about how shoving starts and when it stops being "funny" and starts being thoughtless, even dangerous. Since their report emerged, the number of troublesome incidents has declined. Even faculty members who demanded that it disappear altogether were able to be patient.

Another kind of shoving, however, has been troubling the faculty lately, one subtler but no less injurious than excessive horseplay. It is a kind of shoving which cannot be seen, and this time the students are not coming to their teachers to ask for their protection.

We ask the teachers for examples. The kids are telling each other a lot of unacceptably dirty jokes. In one case, an adult was within hearing distance, and when the wisecracker's friends warned her with their raised eyebrows, the student protested, "Look, she's a lot older than I am. If I can handle it, she can handle it."

However, the issue for the adult wasn't whether she understood the "joke" or even whether she could "handle" it. The question was boundaries, boundaries of good taste, of sensitivity. There was nothing more curiosity-provoking, she knew, than a half-understood joke. Whose job was it to stop such jokes from being told? Whose job was it to explain the joke to the kids? Even more important, whose job was it to put it into context for them?

This particular joke was outrageous. It presumed sophistication about sex. It demeaned specific people and did not even remotely point in any sociably desirable direction. While even young people expect unlikely scenarios in jokes—they know jokes do not describe the literal truth—lurid scenes are likely to stay in their heads. The half-understood situation might fade in their memories, but the images may not. The toxic residue of the joke may become part of their mindset, like scenes from television often appear to do.

Physical shoving can easily be classified as "horseplay." This is something much subtler, something a committee of teenagers might find to be new ground. Here a personal "space," invisible but no less palpable, is being entered without permission. Some of the more sophisticated kids are taking advantage of the less experienced ones. A young person who is made to feel uncomfortable by such jokes is even less able to walk away than he would be if he saw a shoving match further down the hall. Counseling him merely to leave, or to ignore it, or to tell the joke-teller to stop being such a jerk rarely helps. It especially does not work if the youngster who is uncomfortable feels stupid for not "getting" the joke in the first place. Like physical shoving, this controversy involves different definitions of humor and of what might harm a child.

All these ambiguities often make teachers feel powerless to intrude themselves into such situations, even as they fear that these jokes may harm the moral atmosphere of their school. Stopping a joke—with all its likely and unlikely targets—is hard to defend. Often the harm is done by the time the monitor has figured out what is going on. And the teacher's reaction, no matter how moderate, will only make the joke more memorable in the students' minds.

Adults may feel less powerless, however, when students are heard maligning another student, even when it is disguised as a "joke." Stopping the homophobic or racist slur is a more obvious part of a teacher's job description. Even then, however, the teacher needs to admit that he has been eavesdropping, that he has thereby entered the students' personal space, that he insists on their conforming to the moral values of the school. All involved can ask: Who is shoving now?

The answer is both. Both the students who are making the remarks and the teacher who has decided to stop them are shoving. They are entering space into which they have not been invited. They are rushing in where more cautious—less responsible?—souls might fear to tread.

There are different kinds of shoving in a school just as there are different attitudes about the use of threats to promote changes in behavior. In this case—the homophobic remark, leveled toward a student or his family—it is clear where the lines are. Even when students discuss the sexual preference of one of their friends—insisting that they are "not demeaning" anyone, because the friend in fact "doesn't care"—it still is a case of shoving. It is a personal topic and the student being discussed has not brought it up. The natural curiosity of the young has become invasive.

Another form of shoving is rudeness. Rudeness happens when a reasonable difference of opinion or style crosses a line of respect which teachers and students have a right to expect in school. A school is an intentional community; it is not like walking down the street, taking a subway, or shopping in a supermarket. Although a public school ought to be open to the public, it has a right to insist on certain forms of behavior and on mutual respect. Each school must define its line, explicitly or by default.

In most schools, respect is indicated by titles which indicate the roles that various members of the community play. The teacher is called Mr. or Ms., but the student is called Jerry. The principal is called The Principal, the janitor is called Tom, and the cafeteria ladies don't have names at all. Although every member of the community is important to the accomplishment of the school's work, the various titles inevitably indicate that some people are more crucial, and thereby deserving of more dignified respect, than others.

Some schools attempt to eradicate this problem by eradicating titles, but issues of respect never seem to go away. A teacher who had taught for several years came to work in such a school and struggled with the shift from being "Ms. Simmons" to being "Kate":

I never realized that I cared so much about what the kids called me. Are they going to expect me to be a "pal" rather than a teacher? Am I going to have to pander to them? Will they think they know as much as I do about American literature? Is calling me by my first name going to make a difference when I assign homework? In a world without titles, is it the students who be-come "entitled"? Is that the new aristocracy?

Sure enough, the first time a student coolly eyed her when she chastised him for being late to class, she sensed that he was treating her with disrespect. He didn't even attempt to explain why he was late. Indeed, he seemed to feel that it was she who was being rude for expecting him to be there.

Where are all the pillars on which I have built my career so far? Is "class time" as sacred as I have always thought? Do these students believe that the time they spend with me is useful? Do they want to learn what I know? Do they want to improve in the skills which I am able to teach them?

Kate Simmons and her student are both human beings and in that sense, ultimately, equal. Still, she has qualities which he does not have. Besides the fact that she is older and knows American literature, she is a career teacher who has gathered the credentials to make her presence at this school worth pay-ing for.

Is he aware of that distinction? Should I point it out to him? No! He would be offended. He would think I am putting him down, and then he will be even ruder. Heck, he'll think I am being rude, and maybe he will be right!

Schools which explicitly strive to become small "democra-cies" breed such interior dialogues. On one hand, each member of the community is important and must feel as if his or her voice is heard. On the other, teachers will need to have more power than other people or they will not be able to do their jobs. They are their students' keepers: besides conducting classes and assigning homework, they assess students' work. If they don't consider some of it good enough, some students won't pass.

Of course, the kids assess my work too. They constantly talk about which are the "bad" teachers, and their parents talk as if they knew what they were talking about! So does the principal sometimes.

On the whole, Kate Simmons enjoys the confidence of the students in her new school. She herself remembers how shy she used to be, and she feels it held her back educationally. The students here are certainly not like that, especially not in these first few weeks when it is they who are explaining the norms of the school to all the newcomers, including herself.

One of them told me that this was a school where teachers and students were equal. That she would respect me when I had earned her respect, but not until then. No! I can't handle that, but I don't know how to explain myself. Shouldn't I be innocent until proven guilty? Does the principal know that this student feels that way?

As the routines of the class are established, Simmons slowly gains the cooperation of the students in promptness, homework, and general decorum. As in her other school, it takes longer for her to relate to the students out in the hall. Even she feels she is a little shrill there, compared to in her classroom. It's kind of hard not to sound flustered when you don't know a student's name but you have to get him to stop doing something silly.

Some of their behavior offends me, but they tell me there's no rule against it. Are they rude to be kissing in the hallways? Am I rude to be asking them to stop?

After a while, the teacher gets used to being called by her first name. She realizes that, at this school anyway, it implies no disrespect on the fourteen-year-old's part. She remembers, though, how excited some of her former students were when they traveled through the ranks of high school, doing better and better work, and, at graduation, were invited to call her by her first name. They felt as if they had really become her friend in a adult sense—had really achieved something.

*Were they right? Were those worthy hurdles which I was put-
ting before them, or was I really exploiting them? And what about
the people who never called me by my first name? Did they feel less
close to me?*

How close should students and teachers be? If students con-
fide in their teachers, are there areas which should be off-limits,
such as criticizing the teacher's colleagues? When teachers and
students grow fond of each other, is the teacher's judgment im-
paired? What are the necessary boundaries of their relationship? When those boundaries are crossed, is either one of them
guilty of rudeness or of lack of respect? Or even of trespassing,
a form of going where you're not invited?

Usually, the motive behind the schools-as-small-democracies approach is to make those schools more fundamentally *polite* places. If every single member of a community feels valued,
each of them will tend to work hard to safeguard its precious
nature. This will make most members more considerate, more
welcoming to newcomers, more eager to make sure that no one
feels disrespected. No practice is a sure thing, however: for
some students, being "valued" is merely license to do what
they want.

Governing by agreed-upon norms rather than imposed-
from-above rules takes more time. The discussions can seem
endless. Each potential protester, each confused newcomer,
needs to be brought along. Each context, actual or hypothetical,
needs to be described before the school's people can work out
what is considerate behavior, instance by instance. Even this
generous practice can be misunderstood.

The 1990s present young Americans with a host of such instances. Many veteran educators find "rudeness"—casually deliberate disrespect—to be more of a problem in more schools,
whether stereotypically hierarchical or democratic, than what
they observed earlier in their careers.

Most adults are troubled by the adult level of sophistication (or worse) to which children are exposed, on television, in the movies, in rap songs and political life. Limiting their access to it brings up thorny problems of freedom of speech, so we are not sure where to begin. Most of us, parents and teachers alike, are very busy and very distracted and hoping against hope that our children won't ask us to help them to make sense of it, particularly the embarrassing issues. We cling to the statistics which say that children don't really grow more profane or violent or sexually active just because their culture surrounds them with these sounds and images. We try to ignore the statistics which claim the opposite. If we have the opportunity and the money, we sign our kids up for so many extra activities that they will not be able to watch as much television. Whatever we do, it appears that the adolescents have less opportunity to talk to us, and are left on their own.

Teachers can thus count on fewer stable norms to affect adolescent behavior. The variety of childhoods from which the current younger generation arises reflects an unprecedented variety of cultures, a basically welcome reality but an unstabilizing one nonetheless. The frank, harsh popular culture is a further and strident influence. Not surprisingly, many adults are shocked by a rudeness which most students do not even recognize as rudeness.

Rules, strictness, titles, structure may be short-term or even long-term solutions to rude shoving. Nothing, however, will be as effective as the chance to confront and then to discuss all of these important issues. Only then can all the participants design procedures which offer basic respect to every single member of the community and to the idea of community itself. Such discussions are difficult to forward in large and therefore impersonal, overscheduled schools.

A S ALWAYS, a thoughtful curriculum can surface issues of shoving, the "invasion" of one person or people by others. Teachers help their students see that politeness and decorum are not always virtues, but neither is invasion of coveted space. It all depends. Breaking rules or norms is considered a virtue only in cases which are ultimately seen as good causes. It takes discrimination, which is what Samantha is only beginning to develop. She has the right to be confused.

There is an irony here: serious scholarship encourages students to go where they are not invited, to be creative, to "break new ground." Design your own Science Fair project, we say, while you master what has already been learned about chemistry. Develop your own drawing style during your study of other artists. If it is not literally possible at this stage in your lives to "break the mold"—a stunningly aggressive term—at least learn about and admire the mold-breakers of the past. Scholarship is in part about questioning revealed truth and, where demonstrably necessary, replacing it with a new, more persuasive truth. Schools teach their students to admire such scholarship.

Some of the most famous intellectual and scientific heroes, however, were considered by many of their contemporaries to be ill-mannered, egotistical, threatening invaders of already-occupied space. Only well after their offending activity were they lionized. The Church in the seventeenth century had a big "No Trespassing" sign around certain explanations of the universe, but to no avail. The bravest scholars, such as Galileo, marched right in. It was a form of shoving which benefited us all, but he paid for his defiance with house arrest.

The most courageous political leaders have typically shoved in threatening ways. Abraham Lincoln decided to resupply Fort Sumter in the Charleston harbor, though he knew that it would enrage the South Carolinians. Martin Luther King and his followers practiced nonviolence, but they deliberately put Black Americans, even children, into the face of the existing authorities. The shrewd student will note that Napoleon Bonaparte similarly tested all of Europe when he conquered most of it and even marched on Moscow.

Provocative examples of intellectual trespassing and of the varied interpretations of it may also be found closer to our time. In 1998 a nine-year-old student, with the help of her mother, designed a science fair project in which she carried out a test of one of the widely asserted powers of telepathic medicine. She tested the premise of the "therapeutic touch," the idea that healers can sense a patient's "energy field" at a distance of a few inches. In her elegantly simple research design—perhaps agreed to by the subjects of her inquiry because they perceived her to be charmingly naive—a screen, placed a few inches above a table, separated her from the healer she was testing; she simply put her hand over one of the healers' hands and asked them to tell her whether it was their right or left. Their answers were slightly less accurate than they would have been by chance, confounding the conventional wisdom and undermining the integrity of the accepted diagnostic procedure. The youngster not only won a prize at her science fair; her study withstood scholarly scrutiny and her research was reported in a prestigious medical journal. She learned something about systematic research, and she must have learned much from the outraged reaction of the telepathic medical community. She clearly had been cheeky, a questioner of well-established adult authority. Her shoving was the product of principled grappling. It was not rude; it was shoving trying to be constructive and informed, but shoving nevertheless.

Teachers live with the terrible truth that construction may require destruction, that violence may necessarily precede harmony, that what may be perceived as rudeness can be necessary to achieve something of special value.

They share this truth with their students. Teachers may persuasively argue in class, for example, against the wisdom of the students' parents and of the local newspaper, that a local factory *must* upgrade its environmental practices or be doomed. They may propose radical changes to the United States Constitution. Ask students in Rhode Island, for example, to defend the fact that their state has two senators in the United States Congress while California, thirty-two times as populous, also has only two. How come? you ask. There is an answer. What if? you then ask. A senatorial cow is gored. Is that polite or is it rude? Does it deepen a conversation or only make it uncomfortable?

Examples of destruction and of trespassing abound throughout the curriculum. Scientists maim and even kill animals in order to discover how to cure human disease. Tenth graders kill frogs in order to learn about them. The discovery of DNA by Francis Crick and James Watson (as well as by the largely unacknowledged Rosalind Franklin) built on but also undermined the work of earlier scientists. In the United States, violence played a big part in freeing the slaves. The property rights of some were shoved aside to achieve—or to start to achieve—the human rights of others. Harry Truman had to endorse the dropping of the atom bomb in order to end World War II. Or maybe he didn't. Perhaps a student would like to write a paper to dispute that thesis.

This kind of confrontation may be encouraged inside the classroom. Still, it is a certain kind of trespasser that the teachers are trying to create. Many scientists and other scholars may have gone where they were not wanted; many even acted badly toward each other, but they did so with a belief in observable evidence. Adhering to these conventions—courtesy where pos-

sible, documentation in every single case—provides the authority to shove, the opportunity to present findings which test the
orthodox.

Any scholar or budding student who disputes conventional
wisdom should be required to show the same disposition: courtesy and evidence. Defensible shoving requires restraint and
empathy. It plays little with raw power, with being meaner than
someone else. It requires cautious awareness of existing and defensible boundaries and of what those boundaries have come to
mean. Uncertain boundaries were the reason that what Samantha thought was horsing around might have been an offense to
others. The issues are the same, whether in the small world of a
high school stairway or in international politics.

Sometimes destruction and construction have been seen as
part of the same action. Students should examine that. In Hunan province in China, from which Mao Zedong came, hot pep-
pers planted in the roofs grow vines which cascade down the
walls like water spouts, there to be picked and eaten by the children who are walking by. The children's experience of inserting
a peppery fire into their unsuspecting mouths, the Hunanese
have said for centuries, is good for them. They learn to expect
the unexpected, to respect what might have been forbidden, to
overcome temporary pain. "The best scholars and the best gen-
erals come from Hunan," is the old saying. Shoving into the unknown serves to make kids resilient. Violence (the pepper's
sting, and war for the general) and creativity (trying something
new) may not appear similar, but in certain persons they are al-
lied. There is something beneficial as well as tragic in war,
something destructive as well as constructive in scholarship.

The metaphor of "shoving" can also be used, for example,
to illumine academic dishonesty—bluffing at its worst. A person who cheats on a test is entering space which is not his, space
he has not been invited to enter. He has not really earned the

grade he intends to get. Tests are supposedly protected spaces;
they are isolated, quiet, with questions which are new to the
students. The "No Trespassing" sign is posted, with rewards
securely within. One who cheats, pretending to be something
which he is not, is seeking to gain entry into a place from which
he would otherwise be excluded. Or in putting her name on a
paper whose real author is someone else, she is asking her readers to consider her a careful scholar when in fact she has not
earned that designation. These trespassers want credentials
which they do not deserve. Each of them is cutting in line, and
in that sense, they are shoving.

SAMANTHA is an itch, but at heart she is not as bad as she
seems. Skilled teachers will reach her, and with careful and
loving oversight, they will bring her through the obstreperous
confusion of her adolescence. In every school, however, there
are kids who are impossible to reach, no matter how hard the
adults try. They are shoving in a far more dangerous way.

Jane is one of those kids. She lives mostly on her own, occa-
sionally dropping in on an uncle who gives her a meal or two
and a chance to clean up. He doesn't have any money to give her,
but she doesn't need it: she's been selling drugs for a couple of
years. She comes to school fairly regularly, and when she does,
her demeanor is quiet, watchful. She doesn't draw attention to
herself by acting like a bully. She doesn't seem anxious to keep
up with her schoolwork or to get to know any of her teachers.

For a while, some of her teachers try to engage her, but when
she doesn't respond, they put her out of their minds. There are
more obviously interesting kids clamoring for their attention.
They don't want to think about why she still comes to school.

Other teachers, however, more aware of the mores of the
drug culture, believe that Jane has the "look" of a drug dealer,

and they believe that her reason for coming to school is to keep her contacts with her clients. They realize that she will sell more drugs if she looks clean. They know that students, wanting to believe that drug use will not really harm them, are more likely to buy drugs in a locker-swap with a fellow student than to go on the street. These teachers can put two and two together, and some of them do, but they don't know what they can do about it until something comes out in the open.

It's a free country, they keep thinking; one cannot act merely on vague suspicion. So when Jane passes them in the hallway, eyes averted, backpack stuffed, they do nothing about it. Teachers are not narcs, they insist.

In due course, word trickles out that Jane now brings a knife to school, and this word gets back—anonymously, of course—to a teacher. The school has a very strict no-weapons policy, but the members of the faculty are still uncertain about what to do with Jane. Because she has no parents to speak of, because she has never had a probation counselor or a social worker, because there is no teacher in the school who knows her well, some of the teachers feel that they need to deal with her directly. They know that however hard they try to uphold Jane's rights they will seem overwhelming in their questions about a knife brought to school. If they try to find an adult to help her to withstand questioning which may well turn into an interrogation and a search, she will grow suspicious, disappear, and essentially get away with it. Strict due process feels like a luxury under the circumstances. The safety of the other students seems more compelling.

And so they bring her in, and in the most moderate of voices, ask her about the rumor of a knife. They focus on the weapon, not on the need for a weapon, on drugs. And Jane answers them. She needs the knife to cut the bananas in her lunch box. She needs the knife to cut the rope she uses to tie things to the top of her car. She forgot to take the knife out of her backpack the other day. If she knew who told on her, she could explain things better. No, she doesn't have her backpack with her today. No, she doesn't know where it is.

The teachers pull back, pretending to believe her in order to keep her in school. It would be nice to believe her, or at least to believe that she has been scared enough to change her ways. Perhaps the interrogation has knocked some sense into her, so she won't bring a knife to school again. If she believes that the faculty's eyes are on her, she might even cut out her drug sales, at least at school. They don't have proof, and proof is necessary in a democracy. She is just a child in some ways, they tell themselves, and children by definition grow up.

Jane is tougher than that, however. Within weeks she is back to carrying her knife and has even threatened to use it once in school, on a fellow student who had been in arrears. Desperation has made Jane bold and heedless of consequences. She doesn't seem to see any way out of the fix she's in. She cuts out of school, permanently. Telephone messages to her presumed home are unanswered. No student will tell whether he or she knows where Jane is. Jane simply disappears.

Where, ask the teachers, should we be?

Should we have invaded Jane's life forcibly, merely on the rumors (however persistent) about her? Should we have pushed hard on the kids who passed on the rumors to help collar (and thus "save") Jane? Perhaps only peers can reach a person like Jane. Should the school have a corps of responsible kids who would intervene when it seemed appropriate? Would these students be quickly dismissed as Rats? Or would they have been able to make school a force for good in Jane's life?

Jane never "belonged" at school, or at least a conventional school. A smaller place which daily connected the abstractions of classrooms to the work of the world—a school which from the start included a job as well as study—might have served her better.

Belonging is something that every adolescent should expect at a school. Belonging, or the right to belong, is a moral right of adolescence. And no matter how hard she might make it for us, it is not principled to allow an unformed young adult to be a loner, to be out of reach. We should shove ourselves into her life.

SHOVING, defined only in physical terms, is a bad word in schools. Like so many aspects of high school, it deserves a more sophisticated definition. Instead of turning their backs on shoving, teachers should help their students to consider it carefully, creatively, defining its purposes, understanding its contexts, pushing to its interesting extremes. To do so is to use one's mind in a deep moral domain.

6 *Fearing*

A s t h e 11F English students took their seats in Dick Tomasino's class, they knew something was wrong. Tomasino
did not meet them at the door. He stayed at his desk, intently
poring over something. Perhaps it was his grade book. The kids
sat down quietly. This was not going to be an easy day. Tommy
was mad, they figured. He rarely showed it, but today was different.

Yes, he was angry, but Dick tried to hide his frustrated fury.
When the second bell rang, he got up from his chair, smiled at
the class (he knew they sensed something was up) and said,
"There will be a full period test on the Fitzgerald on Monday."

The silence was total. He went on. "Some of you have read
the novel carefully. Most of you have not. Some of you appear
not to know even the simple plot." He paused for emphasis.
"The test will be on the plot and on the meaning of the plot."
He stressed the *and*. "I will grade it carefully, and it will be the
heart of your second-semester grade. Fail this test and you
might fail for the semester." More and utter silence.

Then, from someone, "Jeez, that's not fair."

"It most certainly is fair. Some of you are simply not doing your work. You have four days to catch up. The weekend,
too . . ."

The threat washed over the class.

Jacob twitched. "Will the term grade include the stuff on the first test? Will the first test count?"

"Monday's test will cover everything. That little earlier quiz will count, some. This will be a full period test. You knew it was going to come, and it's coming Monday, and it covers the entire book."

Jacob kept twitching, looking at his desk. Dick could almost hear what was going on his head, the calculations of his chances of getting a good grade. Dick knew he would hit the books tonight and over the weekend.

Byung, however, intently gazed toward the windows, his fingers loosely holding a pencil which he rapped on his tablet top. He rarely sat squarely in his desk and was today, as usual, coiled around the seat and tablet in a twist which for Dick would have been grotesquely uncomfortable. Byung did not find it uncomfortable—or else he was comfortable with the discomfort. Rap, rap, rap. His neighbors periodically stared at him, but Byung paid little notice. He was in his own fidgety world. Dick wondered if Byung even knew what "hitting the books" meant.

Althea looked like she might actually be ill. She sat motionless, as if in a trance. Dick could sense her stiffening posture, the fear gripping her body as if it were wet cement readying to harden.

Herman looked as Herman always looked: loose, friendly, ready for anything whether it was a joke or a story or a test. Easygoing was not the right word to describe him, however. Confident was better; he had a pleasant, unself-conscious assurance. Dick knew that he would max the test, though his prose would wander and his spelling would falter in places.

Phyllis sat still, apparently not comprehending the doom for her that this test portended. She doesn't get it, Dick thought. Or at least she doesn't appear to get it. Phyllis was one about whom Dick especially worried. There seemed to be no life in her, or what life she partook was a cramped one, involving but a few friends and fewer apparent interests. She had neither the good looks nor a flirty manner that, when all else failed, gave girls at the high school some reason to display a tad of confidence. The kids, behind her back, called her dumb, and worse. But who could tell about Phyllis? She appeared uncomplicated, yet at the same time impenetrable. Dick doubted that she had much self-respect buried under that unanimated exterior.

Aneeshya, by contrast, had her plans all ready. She was poring over her notes, seeming to be ordering them. She appeared oblivious to the rest of the class. It was as if she was already at home at the kitchen table, cramming.

After the previous meeting of 11F, Dick's disappointment over the laggards in the class had exploded in the faculty room. "Why are so many of these kids just not doing the work? Even the good kids? What's with this generation? Don't they know that they have to do at least a little work?" The "a little" had acid in it. Dick's colleagues laughed at him and agreed with him. "Sock it to 'em" was the advice of most. "They don't fear you enough."

Fear me? Dick thought. Do I want to be feared? One was afraid of snarling dogs, cancer, terrorists, disapproving in-laws. But not of teachers. No, I want them to love me.

Can they *really* love me if I don't push them? No, they can't, or they shouldn't. Pushing kids is an act of great respect. *I* know that they can be what *they* cannot yet believe they can be. They can do what they don't like to do. So I must push them. But they hate me when I push, and if they think I am harsh they will not trust me and if they do not trust me they will not learn from me. But, but . . . In the long run they will love me for pushing them even though they hated me at the time. Confusing . . .

And so Dick tried a new tactic. "This is what I expect. You will deliver on it on Monday, or else. No excuses. Meet my standard."

So you fear me. You think I am rigid, vindictive. You might even hate me now. So what. You will love me eventually for pushing you because you will need to be able to read carefully and to write well. My threat is an act of love.

But an act of love for whom? Dick asked himself. He had to admit that he craved the short-term relief of seeing 11F hard at work. And even if a threat would not make them learn, fear would make them work, and much of learning was the result of working.

Jacob would actually enjoy the test, or at least the fact that there was a test. It gave him a surge of energy. He could show his stuff. He could do tests. He liked the competition implicit in them. So what if all the teachers thought he was a grade grubber? The corner-cutting of the other kids would be exposed. He would do well. He would be recognized for the scholar he was. Why shouldn't he have this reward? He had earned it. Of course, he would have to make sure that Tommy was scrupulously fair in his grading.

Byung barely knew that Dick had thrown down a gauntlet before the class. What was Monday? What was the next hour? His mind churned, lurching from this to that. Some kids called him dumb, but he could come out with some of the most remarkable things. Then they called him smart. The Ritalin he took kept him in his seat, or so the teachers said. Fitzgerald? Oh, yes, *Gatsby*. A test on Monday. Oh, I guess so. He would look away, tapping again. Byung inside was in agony. Why, why, why am I so . . .

Althea was paralyzed. Why was Mr. Tomasino mad? Doesn't he know that I can't do timed tests? I know the stuff, but tests freeze me up. Monday. Oh, God.

Herman was cool. A test? O.K. He gave me time to study. No sweat.

Phyllis understood that something threatening would roll in on Monday. She knew what a plot was—it's the story—but couldn't figure out what "meaning" was. A story is a story. *Gatsby* was a boring story. Not much happened. Is that what Tommy wants? I'll fail, I suppose. They always expect that I will.

Aneeshya went into high gear. She would get all her notes together. She had kept them carefully. Her mother would have her brothers play outside. "Aneeshya has an important test. She needs to study." I will do well, I will do well . . .

And Ricardo, Janet, and William might show up on Monday and discover that there was a test to take. They were irregularly in class, absent when the *Gatsby* examination was announced. If they arrived, Tomasino would make them take the test. They would write little, slouch, suck their pencils, kid with one another. Tommy would have endlessly to tell them to keep quiet and get down to work. They would obey, but only briefly. They had read but a few pages of the book. It was fun to make fun of English class. The kids laugh. Cool!

Fear works. For some kids. Some of the time.

SCHOOLS EXIST to *change* young people. The young people should be different—better—for their experience there. They should know some important things, they should know how to learn additional important things, and they should be in the habit of wanting to learn such important things. They should have a reasoned, but individual point of view. They should be judicious, aware of the complexity of the world. They should be thoughtful, respectful of thought and of ideas which are the furniture of thought.

Changing young and thus vulnerable people is a deeply moral act, one not engaged in lightly, much less mindlessly. Change can be as painful as it is often exhilarating. Learning can be its own reward, but on other days, one has to push youngsters into learning, to open and to stretch their minds in ways and directions which they may find unimportant or excessively challenging. An important form of pushing is the considered use of fear, with all its challenging connotations.

A paradox of schooling is reflected in the two words, a noun and its qualifying adjective: *unanxious expectation.*

Anxiety drains energy, stifles thought, distracts. Expectations set a standard, give a target, send encouraging signals that a task can be accomplished. Expectations that set a too distant or irrelevant target or a demonstrable threat promote paralysis. At the same time a lack of anxiety can create listless smugness. The trick is to find the right balance between the two. The second trick is to recognize that the right balance will differ among students, from Herman to Althea to Phyllis.

No school can organize itself wholly one by one, with a remedy unique to Byung and an utterly independent approach for Jacob, any more than a family can effectively treat all its members as unique. As a place full of many people, a school's community has to have a recognized posture, some universal norms. The collective middle ground must signal that each person can feel safe, understood as an individual and heard. It must likewise signal that serious work on serious matters is a nonnegotiable expectation. It must be a place where what is demanded is achievable.

Practically, these two threads weave uncertainly. There can be no one best threat, or one best approach to lessening anxiety. The school's routines must be supple enough to allow for a variety of approaches. Aneesha, Janet, and Althea deserve no less. Reasonable adaptation of school routines to the complexity of a young person's learning is a practical necessity and a moral imperative. Not all kids are alike. Not all approaches, whether unanxious or spurred by high expectations, will work with everyone all the time. Standardization of such routines is as inefficient as it is often cruel.

Tommy knows all that. But the School Board did not hire him to teach each student separately. He is teaching a class, and the text is a common one, and the class needs this test. So his expectations will have to be accompanied by their anxiety. At least next Monday.

FEARING FOR oneself is the new kid's lot. The first days at a typical American secondary school are likely to be terrifying. By elementary school standards, most secondary schools are large, and they are centrally administered. Most have a main front door through which the multitudes enter, Grand Central Station at rush hour. If you are young, you are likely to be physically small, compared with the eleventh and twelfth graders. You cower, in the flesh or just in your mind. The big kids all seem full of confident swagger.

There is a homeroom, but one spends little time there compared with the routine at elementary school. Homeroom in high school is mostly the check-in place where the daily bulletin is read. The teacher doesn't say, "Hi, Jim." He reads "Kunkowski?" off his attendance sheet and Jim K. says, meekly, "Here."

The thundering horde follows, filling the hallways with movement and noise again, every fifty minutes. The separate classes in between are full of strangers. There are older students in some of these classes, kids who "failed" and are "repeating." Their braggadocio is brazen. Again, the teachers read names from their lists. "Kunkowski?" The science teacher looks up. "Oh, there you are . . . Landau? Is there an Ann Landau

here? . . ." There isn't the informal time, the chatting, so familiar in elementary school. Here it is all work, and by the numbers.

Scariest are the bathrooms. The smokers hide there, hos-
tilely, furtively. While more welcoming, the cafeteria has its own
perils. Twenty minutes for lunch, and the food lines are slow.
Where can he eat? Jim knows almost no one save some kids who
came up from the elementary school, and they must have already eaten in First Lunch. He spots an older teenager from his
neighborhood. He tries to catch his eye, without success.

So many people from so many races, so many big people, so
many different long halls, so much rushing about from class to
class, so much confusion, so little time: there is plenty of tinder
for anxiety in a high school's simplest routines.

Jim goes home exhausted. He feels as if he will always be an
outsider in that place. He's constantly being told what to do,
and just as constantly being told that he's doing it wrong. After
ten days his mother asks about his teachers. Jim says that they
are okay. "Only okay?" "Well, I don't know any of them very
well." "Do any of them know you yet?" "Nope."

The terrors are not only in the school. He is maturing. He is
beginning to shave, at least once a week. It makes him feel silly,
self-conscious. He senses his sisters snickering at his new
growth. Girls may be interesting in a new way, but he is not quite
sure. Eventually he is expected to have a Girl. The girls know
this and play with his awkwardness. He is flattered and scared,
at once, scared to act on his feelings, scared not to act on his
feelings, scared of being a klutz if he finally acts, and scared that
the girls will laugh at him whatever he does.

School functions as though none of these horrific changes
were happening. The best of what the school officially says is,
"you're on your own . . . you are responsible for the person you
are." And yet the teachers seem to have a clear set of expecta-

tions. All the ninth graders are assigned to read *The Color Purple,* as though everyone is interested in other people's lives rather than in how they seem to everyone else in school. A teacher chastises a class, "Stop being so everlastingly narcissistic!" Jim looks the word up, a big-deal insult for a condition that he did not ask for.

Beyond school, Jim deals with a different set of expectations, those of his peers and of popular culture. He is supposed to admire songs and films which open tantalizing but threatening worlds. All sorts of activities which his parents either counsel against or, more often, absolutely never mention, are the media's stock in trade. Smoking is cool now, including smoking dope. His parents seem increasingly distant, though he thinks they may be scared too. They say, "Jim Kunkowski, you're growing up." What guy doesn't want to be a man? In the movies, the unmarried people have sex but the married people don't. Is that the way it is supposed to be? What do you do with parents and teachers who say, "Don't make love but if you do make love, make it safely"? They can't even say "condom"! So where does that leave me? How can I talk to them?

Jim is also afraid that he is losing ground athletically. He likes to play basketball, and while he was in junior high school, he had one of the best records on the team. Now the other kids seem to be growing faster than he is, and he has grown much more nervous during the games. The coach tells him to calm down all the time, and he's getting a lot more penalties. All his worries are affecting his performance. He may even be cut from the team.

What is the role of fear in growing up? At school at least, Jim Kunkowski may get over much of his anxiety. In time, he may be able to walk up the stairs and into the building without being full of dread. He is likely to get the swing of the hallways and a clutch of friends with whom to eat at the cafeteria. He may even enter the Boys' Room without anxiety. If he has some angularity—a prominent parent, high academic performance, or a deep special interest such as playing the trumpet or being the first-string guard, or a long list of mischief-making—he may be admired, or at least well known. If he doesn't have anything special about him, he will probably be left alone. No one will push him or pull him. He will gradually shed many of the anxieties that terrified him as an entering student. He will find within the school's centralized, and thus depersonalized, scheduling system a safe corner in which to live, doing well but not too well. The most obvious expectation of the school is polite conformity. Everyone is nice. They probably really do wish him well. He is proud that he feels less frightened than he used to. Maybe he has accomplished something.

Fear's usefulness seems to be that one feels so much better when it goes away. Or so Jim comes to think. Until senior year, at least, when he wakes up and wonders what will happen to him after high school. Then it is time to feel afraid all over again.

Does fear have a place in school?

"Fearing" does—that is, fearing of the right kind, fearing what is new, fearing that one may not succeed, fearing the public humiliation if one fails. Fearing and having high hopes for oneself are two sides of the same coin. The fearing which freezes a student up, closing down learning, is counterproductive. The line between the two, veteran teachers know, is a fine one.

Is it moral to invoke fear in another?

Yes, if that fear is clearly in the person's ultimate self-interest. One tells a small child that he will be spanked if he plays with the gas jets on the stove. This is preferable to letting him find out for himself why it is wise to be careful around stoves. One tells a psychologically paralyzed student to "put something down on that paper, *now*, or you will get a zero." This is preferable to letting him give up before he starts.

As a general rule, however, inspiration and encouragement are better tools than threat, in school and everywhere else in life. Further, to save the threatener's credibility, an ill-considered threat may have to be carried out; and when the time comes for carrying it out the admonition can clearly appear inappropriate or harsh. So everyone involved suffers. Threats too often arise from anger, and anger is a poor platform for reasoned decisions.

Easy to say . . .

Teachers have to moderate the process, student by student. Fear can freeze a person or it can energize her. Only a person who knows that student can ascertain which is which. Save at the extremes—there shall be no physical fighting—there are few certain lines to be drawn. Threats sweepingly applied are likely to fail.

That is just liberal mush. Situation ethics. Anything goes . . .

Wait a minute. Life is complicated. One can have standards—thou shalt not cheat by copying another's work without attribution—and still have room (and an obligation) to sort out, in a particular child's case, whether his plagiarism was due to deliberate malice, sloppiness, or ignorance. There must be penalties, but the punishment should scrupulously fit the crime.

So Althea and Herman are different. How can a high school properly cope with those differences?

By so arranging things that Althea and Herman are known well, not just by one teacher but by several. Practically speaking, this usually happens only in a small school or an autonomous small unit within a large building, in which the adults control the time and circumstances of each student's progress.

Knowing a child is not enough. One has to have the authority to act upon that knowledge in the interests of that child. Tightly scheduled schools rarely are supple enough to let this happen. The kids suffer.

Won't this lead to inconsistencies?

Of course. Herman and Althea will not flourish with the same routines. Inconsistency is the mother of universally high-quality work.

That sounds ridiculous.

No more ridiculous than the notion that all patients with ulcers should receive precisely the same medical regimen and will therefore heal at precisely the same rate. It is a nuisance that kids differ, but there is no dodging it.

Making exceptions will be costly.

Indeed. That is why high schools must be administratively very uncomplicated places. The more they take on, usually without full funding for the new initiatives, the weaker the core of their work becomes. They become rigid, dependent on everything going exactly as the finely tuned plan says they should go. Accordingly, there is no give in the system, give that allows for adaptations. Indeed, in many schools "adaptation" is considered aberrant.

Nothing is more important than that each student is known well and that the people who know each student have the authority and flexibility to act on that knowledge.

Surely there are some widely agreed upon standards which schools should rigorously foster. Should not the children be fearful of not meeting these and their teachers fearful of not making that happen?

Certainly. In the academic realm these standards are, at first blush, obvious. The basic purpose of the school is to promote them. That a child can read, write, and cipher, at a useful level. That a child knows something about cause and effect, that what happens first is likely to affect what happens next. That a child knows the routines of democratic government and the restraints that make us free. We should insist on that. Whatever it takes. All of us should be fearful if these obvious democratic skills and attitudes are not well learned by every student.

Beyond those basics, good and decent Americans will always disagree over the particulars. By the time youngsters reach high school, there are more disagreements than agreements. Serious secondary education is about culture, and—whether we like it or not—a society's culture is in constant movement. What is tasteful, what is decent, what is true, what is expected are not fixed entities, to be accepted, implicitly or explicitly, for all time. The Civil Rights movement reminded us that yesterday's common sense is tomorrow's outrage, and vice versa. Check the standard, respected American history textbooks in use in 1950 with those in use in 1980, a mere thirty years later. The lessons therein differ; the test questions which follow will arise from different perspectives. Though the canon of American civil rights has at its core a moral, even religious, conviction, what goes and what does not go for one time is not necessarily the canon for all time.

Situation ethics again. "Nothing" standards.

What is the alternative? Some small group telling all of us what is right and wrong, what is worthy to learn and what is not? The best standards are a habitual attitude of fair and careful analysis (and the tools by which this analysis might proceed), a commitment to defensible truth, and a willingness to consider the previously unconsidered. Simply, disciplined thought, the habit of using it, and the curiosity which leads to endless but essential questions which fuel it.

What does all this have to do with fearing?

A great deal. The culture wars which now infest educational policy are the products of fear. If our children do not know "X," they will fail. Not at life—a good life is created by the right habits far sooner than by the right content—but at the competition for scarce places, the admission to which demand the display of a narrowly defined "X."

We all fear the future. We want moorings, secure fixtures for right and wrong. We want our children to respect these, even to fear a future without them. We wish our children to act in the civil domain with the equivalent of what some churches call God-fearing rectitude. This will give them respect, solidity, and eventually confidence.

Again, the problem is that the world constantly changes, and with it the definitions of what that "X" might be.

How then to choke back our fears?

The only device, fragile though it may be, is to trust our minds, our habit of using them well and our emotional sturdiness. What we need to know may change, but we can insist that we will adapt thoughtfully and well and act accordingly.

Our main fear should be that we will fail to provide the education necessary to create citizens who are in the habit of so using and trusting their minds.

That's a thin reed by which to lessen our fears.

There is none stronger.

D ICK TOMASINO is a decent man and a good teacher, and his dilemma is a common one. He struggles against the detachment which so many of his students feel, detachment attributable at least in part to the large, impersonal high school to which they have been assigned. He realizes that a threat like the one he made will have vastly different consequences, depending on the student, and that some of those consequences will be counterproductive. The best way to motivate the students to do their work in his class would be to have personal credibility with each one of them: not only now, but next week, next month; not only with those who are doing well, but with those who, for a variety of reasons, are doing badly. How can he gain such credibility with a hundred and thirty students to teach every day?

He also knows, because he has taught students like Jim, about the difficulties of growing up in an especially confusing time. He realizes that it's these distractions which make so many students use the shorthand of grades to assess their own progress. The hard, complex, and often puzzling substance of what they are studying requires a focus and a maturity which they don't have.

He has had many dialogues in his head similar to the one above. He knows the pros and cons of tests and of grades. How much should he push his students to see beyond the limits of grades? How can he help his students to measure their own progress? How much should he use grades as motivators, recognize their usefulness as the currency of the realm?

Teachers, like students, have their anxious and their unanxious expectations. Dick Tomasino's expectation is that *Gatsby* is a book which can be read on different levels and that it will benefit his students. His anxiety is both that some of his students will not read it at all, even under the threat of a test—and will then resort to devious attempts to fool him—and that others will freeze under the pressure, writing tests which poorly reflect what in fact they know.

His deliberate use of fear makes him fearful of the consequences for his kids. Letting them slip by him would make him fearful too. In his case, he finds a way to move on from his own fears by analyzing them. He sticks to his plan but individualizes it. Where the plan prods the lazy, he reaps a richer crop of student work. Where it terrifies the innocent, he helps each student to deal with his or her areas of weakness. When he is accused of inconsistency, he smilingly admits to whatever "crime" that might be.

In the end, Dick acts like the pro he is. He practices his craft with bravery, sensitivity, and good judgment. He understands the fears with which each student is dealing, and how great a tolerance each one has for threats. He is able to take each student on his or her own merits, to convey, not a generic hope, not a one-size-fits-all confidence, but the specific version which can only come from the student's own facts, and from knowing each child well.

This is Dick's style of teaching. It can only be sustained when the institution behind him respects and supports it. If he is saddled with a tremendous teaching load, he will adjust his own expectations to accommodate the work he has been given. He will still meet his classes, he will still assign homework, he will still fill out report cards. He will still know his students' names and they will still think he is smart. They will still enjoy his jokes and fondly refer to him as "Tommy" behind his back. On the surface, nothing will be tremendously different.

Underneath, however, he will be a completely different professional. The personal part of Dick's interactions with his students—both on paper and face to face—is the time-consuming part. Time is what he does not have, so it's the personal part which will be sacrificed. He will not know his students well so he will not be able to think of ways to help them. He will need to rely on threat, more and more, to get them to do the most basic work. He will either remain in his job, a shadow of the teacher he meant to be, or he will quit. Other excuses may be found for either option, but they should not fool us. The problem is that we have not been willing to arrange things so that Dick could do his work in a fuller and more time-consuming and effective way. And the fact of the matter is, we could. The students see that, and more than anything else, it brings fear into their hearts, and dispirits them.

AFTERWORD: *Thinking*

T HE STUDENTS are watching.

How we adults live and work together provides a lesson. How a school functions insistently teaches.

If we care about our children's values—how as a matter of *habit* they treat others and how aware they are of why they do what they do—we must look into a mirror. Do we teachers, as a matter of habitual practice, bluff? Do we sort unfairly? Do we treat students harshly in the name of order rather than as a way to promote student growth? Do we grapple over unworthy things? Do we act in a manner which reflects the values which we wish our students to assimilate? What do our actions tell our students about our purposes? About our principles? Have we adopted a style which is insistently moral without becoming moralistic? Do we administrators and policy-makers impose regimens and instruments which are arguably thoughtful and fair?

All this does not mean that each of us consistently must be a paragon. "There is never an instant's truce between virtue and vice." As Thoreau realized, the struggle within the human heart to do what is right and to avoid what is wrong is never-ending. It pops up in unexpected places. It makes us human; in that sense it is our challenge but also our delight. Teachers and administrators are as caught up in that struggle as anyone else. We get angry, cut corners when things are tight, get exasperated. However, if we are honest with them, young people can watch us deal with that and learn (and, we hope, learn worthy things) from the way we regroup and rebuild.

What the young people should not experience is sustained hypocrisy. The school which claims that "everyone can be what he can be" but which demonstrably discriminates or silently tolerates discrimination imposed by higher authorities sends a devastating message: Do as I say but not as I do. No message is more corrosive, especially for teenagers.

As soon as we honestly focus on the "curriculum" provided by the school's daily functioning, we get into a nest of particulars. Morality is not "achieved," like the soccer trophies or the essay contest certificates which stuff the glass cases in the school's front hall. The state of a school's goodness is far more fluid. It depends on what each person brings into the community every year—indeed, every day. A school is prizeworthy if inside every single head—adult and child, producer and consumer—there is a clear reference to principle in every decision and a determination to do the best thing. This is an active process. We are forced to shift from nouns to verbs.

Of course, every school needs its nouns; and even its "nonos." No violence. No theft. No absences. It also needs the processes—the institutional habits—that emerge when those strictures appear to be violated. The verbs emerge from these processes.

"No violence" as a rule is clear until an ambiguous shoving situation arises. "No theft" as a rule enters a fog when someone "borrowed" a book rather than blatantly stole it. Valuing personal credibility collapses when students are shuffled every hour from one class to another, the majority of them effectively anonymous.

This does not mean that a rule stipulating "no violence" is without merit. It merely means that people have to think hard and fairly about its application in a particular situation. This is easy when one adolescent loses his cool and slugs another. That action is clearly wrong. It is more difficult when one considers the "violence" inherent in the taunting of that kid by the person who ultimately got slugged. And the issue gets even murkier if the slugger was a person with very "special needs."

The heart of it all, in school and beyond school, is *thinking* about the practical meaning of absolutes. Such thinking does not necessarily weaken those absolutes. Rather, it deepens them. Civilized people are in the habit of thinking about the reasons for and the consequences of actions, and acting on that thought.

All this takes time, a willingness to struggle, and a commitment to involve students in that endeavor. The formal curriculum, especially but not exclusively in the humanities, is a superb vehicle for this hard work. However, it is critical for a faculty to make the time to consider—again, with the students—the *routines* of a school, why they are needed, what they tell us all about what is more or less principled, what they signify about respect for truth, for differences and for fairness.

Underneath all this is the assumption that principled behavior more often than not springs from actions arising from reflection, from the weighing of alternatives, from the careful specification and definition of affected, even competing, ideas.

Some people seem just to be "born good." In them, there doesn't seem to be much of a struggle; they are serendipitously perceptive and generous. However, the chance for error is always present in everyone. And in reality, most "good" people learn from the many moral lessons which surround them, at home and at school. They are known for judicious decisions because they think hard about the alternatives. They have reasons for committing to things. By taking the time to reflect on (say) how they would value an action if it were to affect them, they are likely to arrive at a more reasonable and principled position than if they only considered its effects on others.

SINCE THINKING hard about matters of principle is so important, we would like it to return to the center of the debate about public education. We will offer three examples.

Outsiders cavil about "dropouts" and demand policies to drive them back into class; yet if most of us spent time in many of the threadbare and mindless schools with high truancy rates, we would be dropouts ourselves. Indeed, dropping out would be a sensible decision. The routines of those schools provide little of the sustenance which potential dropouts need; instead, they provide disrespect and fear. Yet we have visited programs which "work" with vulnerable adolescents. The walls may still be shabby in places, but the first thing which the students speak of are the different routines which make it possible for them to do their schoolwork well. The designers of these successful programs were *thinking*.

Another example. There are more than a few people of our acquaintance who insist that "tough" decisions be made about individual kids on the basis of scores on "rigorous" tests but who expect lenience—they call it "flexibility"—for their own children. We understand and admire this worthy parental concern. The "one-size-fits-all" approach of "objective" testing is a large part of what makes it offensive even to the people who adopt it. We have a hunch, however, that the flexibility, special attention, and choice on which senior policy-makers insist for their own offspring would work in other schools too. If the practices in their children's chosen schools improve the youngsters' long-range learning and life plans more than machine-graded tests do, we should adopt new assessment procedures across the board. Why should children without advocates suffer while other children do not? The obvious justice in this change hardly requires any *thinking*.

Still, though we start with logic, we are not so naive as to believe we can end there. It will require considerable time, money, and political will to offer adequate opportunities to all children. The issue is much broader than mere testing. It goes to the heart of how Americans decide to group their children and to pay for their schools. People who move their kids out of poor schools often do so to get them away from poor kids, even when they explain their actions in educational language. Are the people who send their children to private or affluent public schools because "the classes are small" the same ones who inveigh against "low standards" in those schools which are forced to assign thirty to fifty students to each high school class?

If so, ask them why class size should be a factor for their children but not for other children. Ask them if they believe rich children deserve a more expensive education than poor children do. Ask them why this obvious discrepancy has not been put on any agenda for a decisive remedy. Give them a chance to explain themselves, but insist on clear and principled *thinking* about the effect of social class on the education we are offering to America's children. And if persuasive—"right"—thoughts are there, ask them why "right" actions have not followed.

The hypocrisy is stifling as things presently stand. But we can as a nation, a school, a classroom, move on, if we care enough about what we are doing and about how we are explaining those actions to ourselves.

We return to that student from a poor family who inquired of his middle-class teacher why she chose to work in such a "dump" of a school. The question is as poignant as it is troubling. Given what the student sees around him, is it a bad question? Startling and blunt it might be; but does it clash with reality? If not, why do we Americans tolerate that reality? The students watch our toleration, in such a neglected school and at more affluent places. They must wonder about our priorities and our consistency.

Moral education for youth starts with us adults: the lives we lead and thus project; the routines by which we keep our classrooms, schools, and school systems; the policies we have come to treasure and the times when we have summoned up the imagination and the courage—and the time and the money—to devise even better ones.

The students watch us, all the time. We must honestly ponder what they see, and what we want them to learn from it.

SOURCES

WRITING on matters of morality and moral education goes back into the mists of time. Some of it—one thinks of Confucius and several early Greek thinkers, of the Bible and the Koran—survives in extraordinary ways. Much of it is embodied in stories. Much of it arises from wonder. Why are we on this earth and what obligations does that blessing impose? And terror, too. How can we stave off barbarism? While it might seem that every pebble on this beach has been repeatedly turned over, the quest for understanding persists. It is the ultimate human quest, one without end.

Like most people who have traveled through liberal educations, we touched but a bare splinter of this immense body of thought. Works inevitably blend and twist together, binding as they will onto one another and playing into each of our minds. Our convictions expressed in this book arise to an important degree from this simmering of five decades of pondering. For Nancy the influences have disproportionately come from Asia. For Ted the work of twentieth-century Americans has been most influential.

In recent years, several works have had special influence in the field of moral education. For us a central figure (and close personal friend) was Lawrence Kohlberg. One of his first statements of his theory of the stages of moral development appeared in a volume the two of us co-edited in the late 1960s, "Education for Justice: A Modern Statement of the Platonic Ideal," in *Five Lectures on Moral Education* (Cambridge: Harvard University Press, 1970). Kohlberg also greatly influenced, and wrote an introduction to, Nancy's *Making Decisions: Cases for Moral Discussion* (Independent School Press/Longman's, 1984). Kohlberg's work has provoked and still provokes friendly and hostile criticism. Some early examples of this, as well as an essay by Kohlberg entitled "The Moral Atmosphere of the School," appeared in David Purpel and Kevin Ryan's *Moral Education: It Comes With The Territory* (Berkeley: McCutchan, 1976). A parallel influence on us as schoolteachers during the early 1970s was a different sort of analysis, this drawn from philosophy: John Rawls's *A Theory of Justice* (Cambridge: Harvard University Press, 1971). The central place of *justice* commanded the attention of Harvard colleagues Kohlberg and Rawls and deeply affected our thinking.

Two decades later came James Q. Wilson's *The Moral Sense* (New York: Free Press, 1993). Wilson's arguments gave us courage. "We [Americans] are convulsed," he writes, "by a debate over whether our schools should teach morality . . . Some conservatives argue that the schools should impress upon their students moral maxims; some liberals argue that, at most, the schools should clarify the "value" choices the pupils might want to make. . . . [C]hildren do not learn morality by learning maxims or clarifying values. They enhance their natural sentiments by being regularly induced by families, friends, and institutions to behave in accord with the most obvious standards of right conduct—fair dealing, reasonable self-control, and personal honesty. A moral life is perfected by practice more than by precept; children are not taught so much as habituated. In this sense the schools inevitably teach morality, whether they intend to or not" (p. 249).

Philip Jackson, Robert E. Boostrom, and David Hansen's *The Moral Life of Schools* (San Francisco: Jossey-Bass, 1993) reinforced our view that context was critical. After examining the processes of familiar forms of moral instruction—precepts, rituals, rules, and so forth—their careful research in eighteen elementary and secondary school classrooms persuaded them of the importance of "three less evident forms of potential moral influence": "(1) classroom rules and regulations that govern interactions between and among teachers and students, (2) commonly held assumptions that undergird and facilitate instructional and curricular arrangements of various kinds . . . and (3) the expressive content of actions, objects, and events whose moral meanings are not immediately apparent unless one is accustomed to looking for them." As their fieldwork developed, these three "forms" of moral influence had become "central" to the scholars' work: "We came to see them as crucial to a full appreciation of the schools' potential contribution to the moral makeup of everyone within the institution—principally students, of course, but teachers as well, and perhaps even administrators, office workers, and other employees" (p. 238).

A rush of other recent books deserve careful notice, both because of what they express and for what their popularity says about contemporary worries about the moral health of the young (and, by easy transference, of their elders). William Bennett has published widely, urging us to read again some of the great moral texts. In a way, his angle of vision is similar to ours. In his introduction to *The Book of Virtues* (New York: Simon and Schuster, 1993), he argues that "moral education must affirm the central importance of moral example. . . . For children to take morality seriously they must be in the presence of adults who take morality seriously" (p. 11). We would add, of course, "and in institutions which in their very functioning embody a principled life." Some, however, have found Bennett's selection of stories to be seriously one-sided; Colin Greer and Herbert Kohl published a differing, lively set of moral texts more congenial with progressive thought, *A Call to Character* (New York: HarperCollins, 1995).

Robert Coles has written extensively on these matters for decades. A recent volume is *The Moral Intelligence of Children: How to Raise a Moral Child* (New York: Random House, 1997). His closing chapter in that book—a writing largely made up of stories about children and adolescents whom Dr. Coles has known as a friend or as a patient—is eloquent. Coles recounts Henry James's answer to his nephew's question about what the young man should do with his life. " 'Three things in life are important . . . The first is to be kind. The second is to be kind. And the third is to be kind.' The issue here is the hortatory verb, 'be,' as well as the adjective—the insistence that one find an existence that enables one to *be kind.* How to do so? By wading in, over and over, with that purpose in mind, with a willingness to sail on, tacking and tacking again, helped by those we aim to help, guided by our moral yearnings on behalf of others, on behalf of ourselves with others: a commitment to others, to oneself as linked to others, that won't avoid squalls and periods of seeming drift, but will become the heart of the journey itself, with its ups and downs, a journey that is, after all, the destination—moral commitment given the life of moral companionship" (pp. 195–196). Coles's book could eloquently stand for us as a chapter entitled Being Kind.

Another influential contemporary behavioral scientist is William Damon, whose recent *Greater Expectations: Overcoming the Culture of Indulgence in America's Homes and Schools* makes a careful argument for the creation—or recreation—of moral communities. He argues that such a community "must express its moral voice in ways that build bridges to the interests and abilities of its young people. . . . Building bridges means communicating standards in a manner that young people can understand, engaging young people in compelling activities and experiences that reflect these standards, and conducting relationships with young people in a manner that embodies these standards" (p. 239). Damon's current work focuses on the development of explicit contracts among children and adults, documents which bring to the fore moral issues otherwise left unacknowledged—and in their explicitness thereby teach—and which have consequences. The shape and the seriousness of moral matters is thus clearly placed in the foreground of morally intentional communities.

Amitai Etzioni's *The New Golden Rule: Community and Morality in a Democratic Society* (New York: Basic Books, 1996) has been influential, particularly as Etzioni has constructed a "communitarian" movement to give robust and sustained practice to his convictions. His work especially affected our thinking in the chapter entitled Modeling. Kathy Simon has carefully studied the moral impact of the formal curriculum (*The Place of Meaning* is to be published in 1999 by Yale University Press); her ideas play nicely with the arguments in our chapter on Grappling.

Within professional education, several writers in particular have had recent, wide influence. Edward Wynne has written widely and with passion on the need for character education. John I. Goodlad, Roger Soder, and Kenneth A. Sirotnik edited a series of scholarly inquiries into *The Moral Dimensions of Teaching* (San Francisco: Jossey-Bass, 1990). Thomas Lickona has written and spoken widely about moral education. His central writing is found in *Education for Character: How Our Schools Can Teach Respect and Responsibility* (New York: Bantam, 1991). Thomas Sergiovanni has focused more narrowly on adult leadership in school reform: *Moral Leadership: Getting to The Heart of School Improvement* (San Francisco: Jossey-Bass, 1992).

This list is but a sampler of interesting writing about moral education. While our present book has benefited from much of it, as the foreword explains, our particular sources for this volume have been the voices and actions of countless adolescents and teachers whom we have heard, watched, and known well over the last four decades. There is no technical footnote for all of them, but our debt for the wisdom they knowingly or unknowingly have revealed to us is incalculable.

NOTES

1 *Modeling*

page 4 The Westinghouse Corporation recently decided to cease its sponsorship of the high school science fair prizes. Another sponsor, likely the Intel Corporation, will continue the work.

page 6 The question of whether one is born with such a spark or captures it from experience may be unsettled, but it is clear that the influence of the school is powerful. See Mihalyi Csikszentmihalyi, Kevin Rathunde, and Samuel Whalen, *Talented Teenagers: The Roots of Success and Failure* (Cambridge: Cambridge University Press, 1993).

page 6 "family-like environments in which individuals are valued": Milbrey W. McLaughlin, Merita A. Irby, and Juliet Langman, *Urban Sanctuaries: Neighborhood Organizations in the Lives and Futures of Inner-City Youth* (San Francisco: Jossey-Bass, 1994), p. 216.

page 10 On a typical high school's inadequate attempts to prepare young people to be thoughtful citizens, see Arthur G. Powell, Eleanor Farrar, and David K. Cohen, *The Shopping Mall High School: Winners and Losers in the Educational Marketplace* (Boston: Houghton Mifflin, 1985), chap. 1.

page 10 an invasion of the "contours of another person's mind . . . would be an act of terrorism": A. Bartlett Giamatti, *The University and the Public Interest* (New York: Atheneum, 1981), p. 134.

page 13 "above all, it is expected, that the Master's attention to the disposition . . .": *The Constitution of Phillips Academy* (1778), reprinted in Theodore R. Sizer, ed., *The Age of the Academies* (New York: Teachers College Press, 1964), pp. 77–89.

page 14 "You accept things you cannot control with humor and grace . . .": *Statement of Rights and Responsibilities*, Francis W. Parker Charter Essential School, Devens, MA (1998).

page 14 On "contracts" between the students and school, see William Damon's *Greater Expectations: Overcoming the Culture of Indulgence in America's Homes and Schools* (New York: Free Press, 1995).

page 15 Charles Merrill's one rule was *Don't Rollerskate in the Hallways:* Charles Merrill, *The Walled Garden: The Story of a School* (Boston: Rowan Tree Press, 1982), p. ix.

page 17 "The basic social virtues are a voluntary moral order": Amitai Etzioni, *The New Golden Rule: Community and Morality in a Democratic Society* (New York: Basic Books, 1996), p. 244.

3 Bluffing

page 52 Recent research on teenagers' physiological development and need for sleep: Mary A. Carskadon, Cecelia Vieria, and Christine Acelo, "Association Between Puberty and Delayed Phase Preference," *Sleep* 16(3): 258–262 (1993).

4 Sorting

page 68 Jefferson proposed a public school system in which the best would "be raked from the rubbish annually": Thomas Jefferson, *Notes on the State of Virginia (Query XIV)*, as reprinted in Gordon C. Lee, ed., *Crusade Against Ignorance: Thomas Jefferson on Education* (New York: Teachers College Press, 1961), p. 94.

page 70 There has been substantial recent controversy over the predictive value of what is now called the Scholastic Achievement Test. Most scholars believe that, when calibrated alongside high school grades, the SAT is a responsible predictor of success during the first year of college. The predictive strength of the indicator appears to fall off quite rapidly thereafter. Derek Bok and William G. Bowen have recently looked at these data, at least from the perspective of academically selective colleges, in

The Shape of the River: Long-Term Consequences of Considering Race in College and University Admission (Princeton: Princeton University Press, 1998).

page 70 "One best system" is an aphorism used by David Tyack as the title for his history of American urban education (Cambridge: Harvard University Press, 1974).

page 71 On high schools as "buffets" of various programs, each with its own demands and reputation, see Powell, Farrar, and Cohen, *Shopping Mall High School*, chap. 3.

page 72 See Jeannie Oakes, *Keeping Track: How Schools Structure Inequality* (New Haven: Yale University Press, 1985); Anne Wheelock, *Crossing the Tracks: How Untracking Can Save America's Schools* (New York: New Press, 1992); and Linda Darling-Hammond, *The Right to Learn: A Blueprint for Creating Schools that Work* (San Francisco: Jossey-Bass, 1997), pp. 266–269.

5 *Shoving*

page 89 On the schools-as-small-democracies approach, see Susan M. Lloyd, *The Putney School: A Progressive Experiment* (New Haven: Yale University Press, 1987).

page 90 See Mihaly Csikszentmihalyi and Reed Larson, *Being Adolescent: Conflict and Growth in the Teenaged Years* (New York: Basic Books, 1984).

page 92 The young person's research is reported in L. Rosa, E. Rosa, L. Sarnor, and S. Barrett, "A Closer Look at Therapeutic Touch," *JAMA* 1998:279 (13): 1005–10.

Afterword: *Thinking*

page 117 On the effects of anonymity in a school, see Powell, Farrar, and Cohen, *Shopping Mall High School*, chap. 4.

ACKNOWLEDGMENTS

WE OWE debts to several people in the drafting of this book. The idea for *The Students Are Watching* arose at the suggestion of Wendy Strothman, then director of Beacon Press. Andy Hrycyna and Micah Kleit took over as imaginative editors, and Susan Meigs copyedited our words with thoughtfulness and accuracy.

Our students in Education 178 at Brown in the spring of 1996 visited schools with us to find "moral moments" and, in 1997, examples of "deep understanding." The portraits which we all wrote and discussed after those visits have greatly contributed to the ideas and stories which are recounted here.

Six helpful friends—three of them our children—offered to read our manuscript and provided wonderful suggestions: Barbara Powell, Arthur Powell, Jim Nehring, Lyde Cullen Sizer, Jim Cullen, and Judy Sizer.